CASSELL HISTORY

THE
RENAISSANCE
AT WAR

THE RENAISSANCE AT WAR

THOMAS F. ARNOLD

General Editor: John Keegan

CASSELL

Cassell, Wellington House, 125 Strand, London WC2R 0BB
www.cassell.co.uk

First published in Great Britain, 2001
This paperback edition 2002

British Library Cataloguing-in-publication Data
ISBN: 0-304-36353-7

Cartography: Arcadia Editions Ltd
Designer: Richard Carr
Printed and bound in Spain

Title Page: *The Imperial Army breaks into the French camp at the battle of
Pavia (1525), with the flight of the French king's retinue, a scene from one of a
series of seven Brussels tapestries commemorating the great victory of the
Spanish Habsburg emperor Charles V.*

Overleaf: *An imagined siege scene from a 1570 German treatise.*

Acknowledgements

THE TEACHING OF HISTORY does not always get the publicity it deserves, though its writing would doubtless disappear if it were not for the inspiring work of the classroom professional. My study of the problems of Renaissance military history began almost exactly twenty years ago, in a senior undergraduate seminar on Machiavelli taught by Marcia Colish at Oberlin College. While other students fell for the tripping verse of the *Mandrake Root* or the steel-cold political maxims of *The Prince*, I became fascinated with *The Art of War*, the first and most influential published Renaissance text to wrestle with the problem of reconciling ancient and modern military practice. Professor Colish's encouragement of my interest in Machiavelli the military reformer was material to my decision to try a career of deciphering the wars of four and five centuries ago. Other teachers and mentors also deserve my thanks. William Neil, again at Oberlin, demonstrated the potential majesty of history in his beautifully crafted lectures, always delivered to a packed house, and always applauded. In graduate school at Ohio State I was coached and prodded by two military historians in particular, Williamson Murray and John Guilmartin. Above all, I thank Geoffrey Parker, my senior colleague in my first years at Yale, who has done more than any other to sustain my career as a historian of Renaissance war.

This book is not mine alone. Its editor, Penny Gardiner, shepherded the project with grace and wit, Malcolm Swanston turned ideas and sketches into marvellous maps, and Richard Carr artfully blended text and images into a whole. I thank them all.

Finally, my wife Tiffany merits special acknowledgement: for her steadfast felicity, and for her daily sufferance of the author's fascination with the wars and battles of long ago and far away.

THOMAS F. ARNOLD
New Haven

Contents

January 1592: (10)
Parma's army gathers at
Amiens to relieve siege
of Rouen

sburg
s

KEY TO MAPS

Military units–types

infantry

cavalry

Military movements

→ attack

⇢ retreat

General military symbols

✕ site of battle

🏰 stronghold

⊙ siege

➤ field gun

Geographical symbols

urban area

urban area (3D maps)

— river

--- seasonal river

⊔⊔⊔ canal

--- internal border

— international border

e Havre

20–21 Ma
Parma
Seine to
avarre and
the Neth
without

No

5 Ju
Nava
omm
t St
leau
s

orbe

Fc

4

Le Mans

5 21 November 1589:
Navarre enters Tours,
his provisional capital
as Henry IV of France

● Orléans

F R A

● Blois

Map list

Chronology of the Wars

1453	
29 May	Constantinople falls to Mehmed II 'the Conqueror'.

1476	
2 March	Swiss Confederacy defeats Duke Charles 'the Bold' of Burgundy at Grandson.
22 June	At Morat, the Swiss again defeat the Burgundians, sealing the reputation of the Swiss infantry as the best in Europe.

1480	
11 August	Ottomans seize Otranto in heel of Italy; expelled in 1481.
23 May – 17 Aug	Failed Ottoman siege of Rhodes.

1481	
3 May	Death of Mehmed II 'the Conqueror'.

1494	
6 March	Charles VIII of France arrives in Lyons to lead his army into Italy to take kingdom of Naples.

1495	
22 February	Charles VIII's army enters kingdom of Naples.
1 April	Formation of anti-French 'Holy League' eventually consisting of the Pope, Venice, Emperor Maximilian I, and King Ferdinand of Aragon.
6 July	Charles VIII fights Holy League at Fornovo during retreat from Italy.

1497	
25 February	Fall of last French possession in kingdom of Naples.

1498

7 April	Death of Charles VIII; Louis XII King of France.
20 May	Vasco da Gama reaches Calicut in India.

1499

10 April	Louis XII defeats Duke of Milan, seizes duchy.
11 November	Treaty of Granada partitions kingdom of Naples between Louis XII and Ferdinand of Aragon.

1502

June	Ferdinand of Aragon begins war to evict French from Naples.

1503

21 April	Spanish general Gonzalo de Cordoba defeats French at Cerignola.
29 December	Gonzalo de Cordoba completes defeat of French at Garigliano river.

1504

1 January	French evacuate kingdom of Naples on terms.

1508

10 December	Anti-Venetian League of Cambrai includes Louis XII of France, Emperor Maximilian, and Ferdinand of Aragon.

1509

14 May	French smash Venetians at battle of Agnadello in Lombardy.

1511

4 October	Anti-French 'Holy League' includes the Pope, Venice, Henry VIII of England, Ferdinand of Aragon, Emperor Maximilian I and Swiss Confederacy.

1512

11 April	Gaston de Foix killed leading French to victory over Spanish–Papal army at Ravenna.

1513

6 June	Swiss defeat French at Novara; French lose Milan.
16 August	English victory over French at Guinegate, also known as the 'battle of the spurs'.
9 September	English defeat Scots at Flodden.

1515

13 and 14 Sept	Francis I of France defeats Swiss at Marignano, winning control of duchy of Milan.

1517

22 January	Selim II defeats Mamelukes, completing conquest of Syria and Egypt.

1519

12 January	Death of Emperor Maximilian I.
28 June	Charles V elected Holy Roman Emperor.

1521

3 January	Pope excommunicates Luther.
13 August	Cortes takes Tenochtitlán in Mexico for Spain and Charles V.

1522

29 April	Imperial Army under Colonna defeats French at Bicocca in Lombardy.
26 June – 1 January	Ottomans take Rhodes.

1524

30 April	French defeat at the Sesia in Lombardy.
30 May	Beginning of German Peasants' Revolt in Black Forest region.
12 Aug – 29 Sept	Failed Imperial siege of Marseilles.
26 October	Milan falls to Francis I.

1525

24 February	Imperial Army defeats French at Pavia; Francis I captured.
15 May	Defeat of German Peasants at Frankenhausen.

2 June	Major defeat of German Peasants at Königshofen.

1526

14 January	Francis I cedes all of Italy to Charles V by the Treaty of Madrid.
17 March	Francis I returns to France.
22 May	Anti-Habsburg League of Cognac including France, the Pope and Venice.
26 August	Süleyman the Magnificent smashes Hungarians at Mohacs.

1527

6 May	Imperial Army begins sack of Rome.

1528

July	Andrea Doria switches Genoa from French to Habsburg allegiance.

1529

19 April	German Lutheran princes 'protest' against majority decision at Imperial diet in Speyer to condemn Lutheranism (the origin of the term Protestant).
23 Sept – 14 Oct	Failed siege of Vienna by Süleyman the Magnificent.

1530

22–24 February	Pope Clement VII crowns Charles V Holy Roman Emperor in Bologna.
12 August	Florence capitulates to besieging Imperial Army; Clement VII Medici restored to power.

1534

24 July	Francis I orders creation of seven new infantry legions.

1535

24 June	Military collapse of 'Anabaptist Kingdom' of Münster.
21 July	Tunis falls to Charles V.

1536

February	Francis I occupies Savoy.
Easter Monday	Charles V, in St Peter's in Rome, challenges Francis I to a duel to settle their political and personal differences.

1537

18 August – 6 Sept	Failed Ottoman siege of Venetian Corfu.

1538

10 August	Ottomans take Spanish-held Castelnuovo in Montenegro.

1541

31 October	Charles V evacuates failed effort to take Algiers.

1542

March	Alliance between Francis I and Süleyman publicly known.

1543

6 September	Turks sack Nice with French co-operation.

1544

14 April	French victory over Imperial Army at Ceresole in North Italy.
17 August	St Dizier falls to Charles V.
14 September	Boulogne falls to Henry VIII.
9 October	French fail to retake Boulogne by camisade.

1545

13 December	Opening session of Council of Trent; formal Catholic Reformation begins.

1546

18 February	Death of Luther.

1547

24 April	Charles V defeats German Lutheran princes of the Schmalkaldic League at Mühlberg.

| 27 January | Death of Henry VIII. |
| 31 March | Death of Francis I; Henry II crowned King of France. |

1549

| 27 August | Pro-Catholic Kett's Rebellion in southern England destroyed at Dussindale. |

1552

15 January	Alliance between Henry II and the German Lutheran princes.
10 April – 26 July	Henry II seizes Metz, Toul and Verdun.
19 Oct – 1 Jan 1553	Failed Imperial siege of Metz.

1553

| 20 June | Thérouanne retaken by French. |

1555

17 April	Montluc surrenders Siena to Spain and the Medici.
15 September	Peace of Augsburg recognizes right of rulers in Holy Roman Empire to determine between the Catholic and Lutheran faiths in their territories.
25 October	Charles V abdicates his rule in the Netherlands.

1556

| 16 January | Charles V abdicates his rule in Spain; his son becomes King Philip II. |

1557

| 10 August | French defeat by Imperial Army at St Quentin. |

1558

6 January	Calais taken by French from England.
14 March	Charles V's brother Ferdinand becomes Holy Roman Emperor.
13 July	French raid in force defeated by Spanish at Gravelines.
21 September	Death of Charles V.

1559

3 April	Treaty of Câteau Cambrésis between France and Spain.
30 June	Henry II mortally wounded at joust in Paris to celebrate Treaty of Câteau Cambrésis; he is succeeded by Francis II.

1560

5 December	Death of Francis II; Charles IX crowned King of France.
21 December	Catherine de' Medici becomes regent of France.

1562

1 March	Massacre of Huguenots at Vassy opens French Religious Wars.
19 December	French Catholics defeat Huguenots at Dreux.

1563

18 February	Assassination of Duke Francis of Guise.

1565

20 May – 8 Sept	Failed Ottoman siege of Malta.

1566

20 August	'Iconoclastic Fury' in Antwerp.
6 September	Death of the sultan Süleyman.
8 September	Ottomans take Sziget.

1567

26 September	Failed Huguenot attempt to kidnap French royal court.
10 November	Catholics and Protestants fight at St Denis outside Paris; Huguenots give up blockade of city.

1568

23 May	Louis of Nassau defeats Habsburg Army at Heiligerlee.
21 July	Duke of Alva crushes Orangist rebels at Jemmigen.

Christmas Day	Revolt of Alpujarras Muslims in in southern Spain against Christian rule.

1569

13 March	French Catholics defeat Huguenots at Jarnac.
3 October	French Catholics defeat Huguenots at Moncontour.
2 December	French Catholics take Huguenot town of St Jean d'Angély.

1570

22 July – 9 Sept	Turkish siege of Nicosia in Cyprus.
15 September – 1 Aug 1571	Ottoman siege of Famagusta in Cyprus.

1571

7 October	Ottoman naval defeat at Lepanto by allied fleets of Spain, Venice and Pope.

1572

1 April	'Sea Beggars' take Brill, reigniting Dutch Revolt.
24 August	St Bartholomew's Day massacres in France.

1573

11 Feb – 6 July	French Catholic siege of Huguenot town of La Rochelle.
13 July	Haarlem surrenders to Duke of Alva; most of garrison massacred.

1574

14 April	Spanish victory over Orangists at Mook.
30 May	Death of Charles IX; Henry III King of France.

1576

3 February	Henry of Navarre escapes French royal court.
May	Beginnings of French Catholic or Holy League.

1578

3 August	Crusade of King Sebastian of Portugal annihilated by sharif of Morocco at Alcazarquivir.

1580

25 August	Lisbon falls to Spain; Philip II of Spain absorbs Portuguese empire.

1584

10 July	Assassination of William of Orange.
31 December	Guise faction in France allies with Philip II of Spain.

1585

17 August	Antwerp falls to Duke of Parma.

1587

20 October	Henry of Navarre defeats Catholic League at Coutras.

1588

12 May	'Day of the barricades': Paris rises in support of the Catholic League and the Guise.
8 August	English fireship attack disrupts Spanish Armada.
10–12 August	Spanish Armada misses its rendezvous with Parma's army, embarked in Flanders.
23 December	Duke Henry of Guise assassinated by order of Henry III.

1589

1 August	Henry III assassinated; Henry of Navarre now has best dynastic claim to throne of France.
4 August	Henry of Navarre declares himself Henry IV of France.
21 September	Henry of Navarre defeats Catholic League at Arques.
31 October	Navarre attempts to take Paris by escalade.

1590

14 March	Navarre defeats Catholic League at Ivry.
7 May – 11 Sept	Navarre besieges Paris.
19 September	Duke of Parma enters Paris in triumph.

1591

11 November – 20 Apr 1592	Navarre besieges Rouen.

1592

2 December	Death of Alessandro Farnese, Duke of Parma.

1593

25 July	Henry of Navarre accepts Catholicism.

1594

27 February	Navarre crowned Henry IV of France.

1598

13 April	Edict of Nantes grants Huguenots right to worship.
2 May	Peace of Vervins between France and Spain.
13 September	Death of Philip II.

1600

2 July	Maurice of Nassau defeats Spanish Army at Nieuport.

1601

15 July – 22 Sept 1604	Spanish siege of Ostend.

1603

24 March	Death of Elizabeth I.

1609

9 April	'Twelve Years Truce' halts war in the Netherlands.

1610

14 May	Assassination of Henry IV.

INTRODUCTION

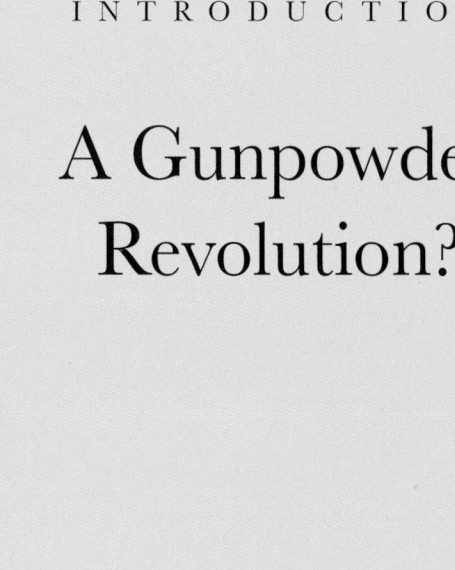

A Gunpowder Revolution?

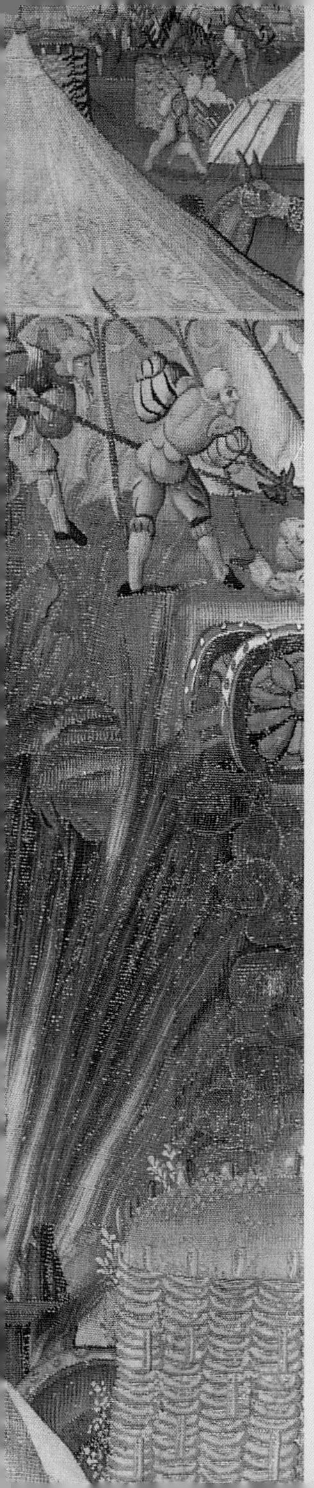

An explosion at the battle of Pavia (1525), a detail from a Flemish tapestry, c. 1530. *Gunpowder brought a new excitement, power and danger to the European battlefield. That was true of other Old World battlefields as well. Even before it reached Europe, gunpowder was an accepted, if supplementary, tool of war in China, India and the Middle East. But only in Europe did a radically different new form of warfare develop in association with gunpowder weapons – only Europe experienced the transformation of a military Renaissance.*

A Gunpowder Revolution?

GUNPOWDER CHANGED WARFARE, and in so doing it changed the world. Of course – but how, exactly?

Traditionally historians have tended to play gunpowder as a technological wild card, a radical new tool of war with enough kick to almost single-handedly knock the Middle Ages into Modern Times. The familiar thesis fits in a nutshell: gunpowder weapons – cannon and man-portable guns – were simply too powerful for ancestral ways of war based on horses and lances, castles and catapults. And as gunpowder exposed the deficiencies of medieval warfare, so the supporting social and political order collapsed as well. The classic opening scenes of this textbook revolution come easily to mind, as clean and sharp in the imagination as a series of steel engravings in a confident nineteenth-century tome. Here in the first scene a grimy-faced bombardier bends over his big-bellied cannon, poised to send a great stone ball smashing into a centuries-old castle, an elegant confection of pointy towers and steeply pitched roofs. With that ball, we understand, this gunner is knocking down a way of life – a way of power – as well as reducing a gothic charm to a pile of splintered masonry. Here is the second scene: the bombardier's country cousin, a handgunner, pops up from a foreground ditch and hedgerow, quick with his finger and eager to knock, in the middle distance, a well-born and well-armed (but not so well-armoured) knight from his finely caparisoned mount. A third scene reveals the economic cause behind the previously illustrated battlefield effects: in velvet hose and with fur at his collar (as well as the heavy chain with seashell pendant of the Order of St Michael), the king's paymaster, a man of soft hands and subtle mind, supervises the distribution of wages to a crowd of mercenary hirelings, including the bombardier and the handgunner. Invisible, but manifest in the clinking coins that bear his royal face, is the lasting victor in this Story of Gunpowder, the monarch. Thus the military, the political and the economic all satisfactorily converge. So say the scenes – and each vignette is true enough. Cannon did tumble many a feudal lord's castle, materially encouraging that nobleman's descendants into becoming first loyal courtiers to the king and then, a few hundred years later, casino operators and husbands to movie stars. And a few pence worth of lead did drop many a proud and expensively equipped knight dead at the feet of his own horse. And royal power did wax as noble power waned. But gunpowder, *deus ex machina*, did not swoop down from heaven – from China, really – to turn medieval Europe on its head.

The full history of gunpowder is complex, and not independent from other events and issues. At the heart of the matter is a general problem

The King of France lays siege to a city, in an illumination from a fifteenth-century manuscript. In the centre foreground a gunner gingerly uses a red-hot poker to touch off a bombard constructed of wrought-iron bars held tight by iron hoops. Though crude by later standards – note the simple trestle cradles – by the mid fifteenth century such cannon could easily smash tall, thin medieval walls. To the left of the bombardier an early handgunner loads his weapon, a small barrel bound to a stick.

of technology in history; namely the fact that invention alone is rarely, if ever, sufficient and necessary enough in itself to force any broader social or political revolution. More important – more powerful – than any new item of technology is the place of that technology in the minds of its users. People, not things, make revolutions. Sometimes a society seizes upon the widest possibilities of technological change (as with the steam engine in nineteenth-century Britain, or with the computer in our own times) and everything is made anew: ways of thinking and ways of doing are transformed for ever. But surprisingly often – surprising only in hindsight, of course, and from the perspective of our own culture – what we easily identify as a potentially revolutionary new technology sparked no great chain reaction of cultural, political or social change. Sophisticated societies sometimes fail to make the choices that we find obvious.

For example, in the Roman Empire experimentation with vacuum and steam power produced only tricks and toys, such as automatic temple-door-opening machines; and Roman watermills, though apparently powerful and useful, remained rare: despite a fertile combination of theory, wealth and materials, there was no late antique industrial revolution – who, after all, in a world of abundant slave labour and complacent landed élites would have sought such a revolution? Even in military history, a field often reduced to weapons lore, new technology alone – even radical and powerful new technology – is never the whole of the story. Put simply, it can happen that new weapons, even potent new weapons, supplement and replace the old without inspiring or forcing any fundamental re-evaluation of warfare.

Such was the case of gunpowder in gunpowder's homeland, China. By the middle of the ninth century AD Taoist alchemical philosophers pursuing life-extending elixirs had perfected the recipe for a magically explosive mixture of charcoal, sulphur and saltpetre: gunpowder. Over the next four hundred years Chinese technicians progressively developed whole new families of weapons based on the smoking, stinking, bursting stuff: flame-throwing 'fire lances'; exploding grenades and larger, catapult-launched bombs; shrieking rockets; man-portable guns, and, by at least the end of the thirteenth century, bulbous metal vessels that must be considered the first true cannon. This march from exploding powder to effective artillery was an impressive, sustained technological achievement – but it did not materially challenge the long-standing traditions of Chinese warfare, or alter the overall patterns of Chinese history. Why not? Perhaps most importantly, China's ruling bureaucrats, in their serene confidence that power would always be rooted in the ancient literary and philosophical classics, remained essentially aloof; the mechanics of warfare were beneath their interest. Also, imperial China remained just that: imperial. With authority ultimately flowing from the central court – literally flowing from the pens of the scholar administrators – no class or community there was tempted or inspired to fundamentally rethink military affairs.

Circumstances were far different on the other side of the globe, in Europe. There assertive burghers, ambitious princes and proud, militant nobles all existed in fractious, competitive, war-making plenty; there was no true controlling political or social centre – no imperial Rome or Peking – to guide the affairs and thoughts of late medieval Europe. And by the fifteenth century, just as gunpowder was finding a place on the European battlefield, Europe's cultural élite – its thinkers and rulers – had gained the confidence to engage in the wholesale redefinition of their institutions, beliefs and practices: the Renaissance. Gunpowder was one of many seeds of change in this restless, unsettled, but also curious and confident world. Across the same decades during which Alberti rewrote the rules of painting (1435), Gutenburg helped introduce book printing (*c.* 1455), Columbus reached America and da Gama India (1492 and 1498), Luther successfully challenged the Catholic Church (from 1517) and Copernicus declared a solar-centric universe (1543), European military experts – engineers, captains, interested intellectuals – similarly rethought and remade the art of war.

Given the ferment of the age, it would have been surprising had warfare evaded investigation and reform. It did not. By the middle of the sixteenth century European war was very different from what it had been a century before. Knights had become officers, and armies were no longer led by heroes but were directed by generals. Infantry marched in step and drilled in ordered formations of ranks and files. Fortress and siege engineering alike depended on exacting and precise geometric rules. And as the techniques of European warfare changed, so did its underlying spirit. War, it was assumed by the middle of the sixteenth century, could be organized and analysed; it was reducible to theory and formula, it could be made into a science and set down in treatises. The whole of this change – mental, technical and material – amounted to a military Renaissance, a revolution in the practice of war that was no less profound than the simultaneous transformations

taking place in the arts and in religion. The proliferation of gunpowder weapons was a component of this military revolution but not its cause – the real cause was the deep Renaissance habit of rethinking anything and everything, including war. And that habit, of course, was applied to the possibilities and problems of gunpowder as a tool of war.

The siege of Paris in September 1590, a painting from the 'Hall of Battles' in the Escorial, the monastery-cum-palace headquarters of Philip II of Spain. Paris was besieged by Henry of Navarre, the Huguenot Protestant claimant to the throne of France. Relief of the siege by a Spanish army led by the Duke of Parma was one of the last military successes of Philip II's reign, and one of the very few that followed the disastrous Armada year of 1588.

Secor0 de
·1· Paris,
·2· Lingni ,
·3· S Clou ,
·4· El campo del Rè de
·5· El Pª de Parme

CHAPTER ONE

The New Fury

A Swiss army uses gunpowder weapons against the Duke of Burgundy, from a manuscript of the early 1480s. At upper left a laager of wagons mounting small cannon helps protect a body of Swiss infantry armed with halberds and handguns from a potential cavalry charge. In life such war wagons were much taller than shown, easily capable of housing a pair or more of soldiers. The prominent bear flag is the standard of the city canton of Bern. In the foreground Swiss artillerists, identifiable by the cross device on their chests, aim and adjust small bronze cannon to fire against the Burgundian army on the opposite side of the river. After their victory over Duke Charles 'the Bold' at the battle of Grandson in 1476, the army of the Swiss confederacy captured over four hundred Burgundian artillery pieces. The wagons and cannon shown here might well have been part of that haul.

The New Fury

THE SECRETS OF both gunpowder and cannon passed to Europe between the middle of the thirteenth century and the first quarter of the fourteenth. Around 1250 the Franciscan Roger Bacon described firecrackers, perhaps brought overland along the silk road from China through Central Asia. Evidence of cannon comes from 1326, with an English manuscript illustration of a bulbous, vase-like weapon lying on a trestle table discharging a feathered bolt against a tower gate. Another, less well known illustration from the same manuscript shows an apparently larger weapon of the same pattern mounted on a sled. Both weapons look very odd to anyone familiar with later Western cannon, but their striking similarity to contemporary Chinese guns hints that their design had passed directly from China to Western Europe, and was not home-grown or based on Arab or Byzantine models.

These first European cannon were certainly more of a pyrotechnical flourish than fearsome instruments of destruction. They joined the

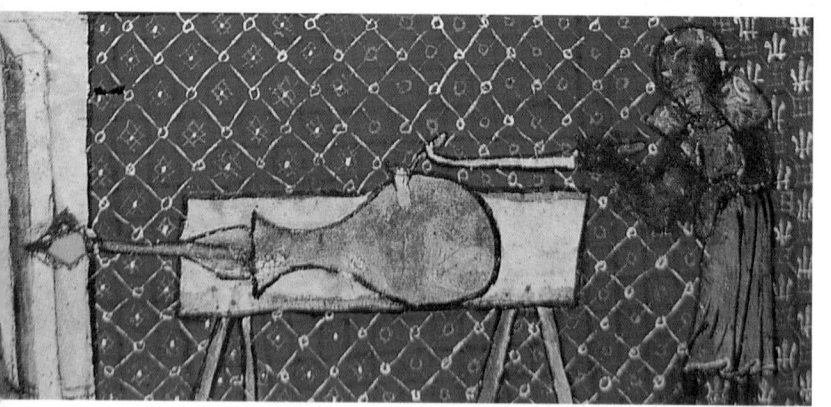

The earliest European depiction of a cannon, from an English manuscript of 1326. This vase-shaped weapon is very different from later Western artillery, but quite similar to some Chinese guns of the late thirteenth century. Both the idea of cannon and the formula for gunpowder may have reached Europe directly from China, carried westward along the 'silk road' caravan route across Central Asia.

battering rams, assault towers and other simple engines of medieval siege warfare, but their effective contribution long remained minimal. The real wall cracker and tower breaker of the later Middle Ages was the giant counterweight catapult, the trebuchet. This was a massive machine of awesome power, the apotheosis of a mechanical artillery tradition reaching back to the Hellenistic age (and including the Arab and Chinese worlds, where the trebuchet was probably first developed). The largest trebuchets stood the equivalent of five storeys tall, their whirling vertical arms lobbing stones of stupendous weight; sources, almost certainly exaggerating, mention missiles of over 1,000 kilograms – but missile weights of a few hundred kilograms are entirely probable. Range and accuracy were impressive, too; the big engines could have thrown a shaped stone of a few dozen kilograms well over 200 metres, and tests with reconstructions have revealed that the trebuchet was a remarkably consistent weapon, able to repeatedly pound the same spot of a target wall. Next to these super catapults the first gunpowder artillery was a flashing, smoking novelty – noisy and exciting, but not much else.

Despite its initial feebleness primitive cannon captured the imagination of Europe's military artisans, who coaxed the new gunpowder artillery past its mechanical competition. Cannon eclipsed the trebuchet in northern Europe around the middle of the fifteenth century, and a generation later in the south – the last records of its use in Europe come from the sieges of Rhodes in 1480 and Malaga in 1487 (where a Castilian engine tossed the body parts of a Moorish suicide assassin into the city). Memory of the giant catapults lingered into the 1500s. Engineers continued to include them in their books of marvels (among other designs, Leonardo da Vinci sketched an immense crossbow mounted on six great wheels), and in the summer of 1521, during Cortes's siege of Tenochtitlán, his desperate artificers, driven by a shortage of gunpowder, built a catapult on top of a captured Mexican pyramid to rain missiles down on parts of the city still held by the indigenous defenders – but the Spanish artillerists could not get the weapon to work properly. Against this failure the same resourceful conquistadors later successfully concocted gunpowder from scratch (they harvested sulphur from a live volcano) and even made cannon from local iron deposits. The old knowledge had been lost; the new age was a gunpowder age.

The fifteenth-century victory of cannon over catapult was the result of both steady technical progress and a growing cultural fascination with guns. Gunpowder became cheaper, as its makers puzzled out better ways of extracting and purifying its chemical components, the most elusive and expensive of which was saltpetre, imported from India, scraped from basement walls or stewed in festering piles of dung, urine, lime and oyster shells. Gunpowder also became more powerful – and more reliably powerful. Corned powder, made by wetting the mixture during manufacture and drying it in lumps or granules, was both more sharply combustible and more resistant to moisture and separation, and thus degradation, over time and during transport. Cannonballs, at first laboriously carved from stone blocks (as were trebuchet shot) became iron in the larger calibres and lead in the smallest. Metal shot were stronger and heavier than stone balls of the same size, and so were more effective at breaking masonry, but stone shot survived surprisingly long, particularly for use at sea – stone-shooting perriers have been recovered from Armada wrecks, and a late sixteenth-century Italian recommended short, light, breech-loading guns firing 20-pound stone shot as useful aboard ships and galleys.

Gunmakers meanwhile honed their craft. Across the fifteenth and into the sixteenth century there were two parallel technologies of cannon manufacture: one of wrought iron, and a second of cast bronze. Forged iron guns were constructed in two layers, like wooden barrels, with an inner tube of long iron staves joined edge to edge held tight by a reinforcing outer casing of iron hoops. Bronze cannon were cast whole, borrowing the methods used to cast the great bells of Europe's cathedrals – a widely dispersed industry. (This knowledge was of comparative advantage over the Muslim world, where the cacophony of church bells was considered one of the scandals of the Christian West.)

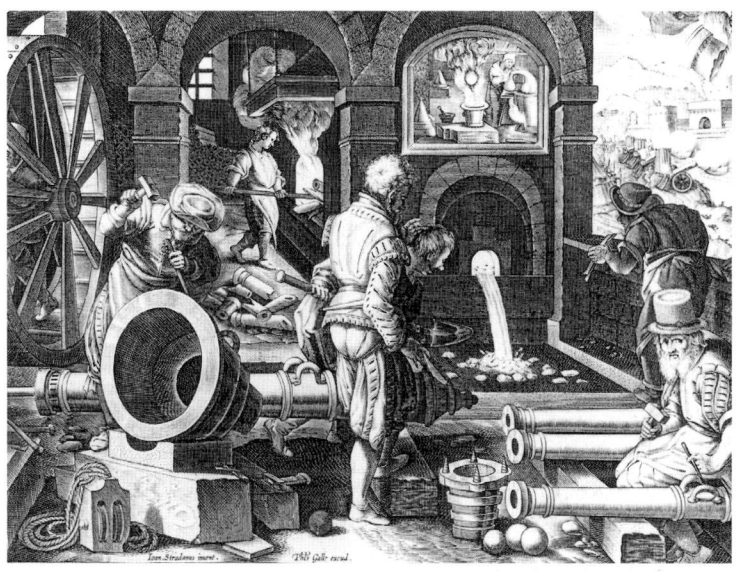

A sixteenth-century engraving of a cannon foundry, by Stradanus. In the centre a well-dressed master supervises the discharge of molten bronze into a casting pit. Notice the broken scrap cannon being loaded into the furnace for recasting. In the lower right a worker uses a hammer and chisel to clean up a freshly cast small artillery piece. To the left of the master another worker similarly chisels away at a medium-sized mortar. In the upper left corner a worker turns the treadmill that powers a barely seen horizontal boring machine being used, in the lower left centre, to scrape a cannon bore true.

The connection between bells and cannon even had a political extension, since the raw metal and manufacturing techniques of the two were interchangeable. In the late fifteenth century, rebel towns subdued by the Duke of Burgundy had to surrender their church bells, and a hundred years later, as parishes in south-east France turned Protestant, the Duke of Savoy cheaply bought up abandoned bells – now rejected as idolatrous – and melted them down to make cannon; cannon he then used to enforce his Catholic authority over the same communities.

Both iron and bronze guns had their advantages. Wrought iron was as much as ten times cheaper than bronze, but whole-cast bronze pieces were safer, less likely to murderously burst asunder – allowing and

A German woodcut of sixteenth-century cannon types. In the foreground an artillerist, with rammer in hand, inspects the muzzle of a large bronze cannon. Since they were important display items for princes, cannon were often cast with decorations at least as elaborate as the example in this print. Tellingly, cannon cast for the austere republic of Venice were comparatively plain. The artillery in the background of this print are a mortar on an elevating platform, two other large cannon and an organ gun with three small barrels. The litter of cannonballs, tools and other equipment – including a drum – is indicative of the massive amounts of material demanded by artillery in the field.

encouraging a gunner to use a larger and more powerful powder charge. Since they were piece-built, wrought-iron guns probably became weaker with age as successive firings shook them apart. And rust was always a threat. Bronze casting, a sculptor's technique, also allowed for elaborate artistic treatment – not a light thing given that cannon were potent display items for Renaissance princes obsessed with prestige. Cast-bronze cannon masqueraded as antique fluted columns; muzzles sported lions' or serpents' mouths, and barrels carried escutcheons, mottoes and makers' marks. From the end of the fifteenth century the advantages of bronze, material and otherwise, increasingly won out, and in the sixteenth century wrought iron was generally only used for smaller, often breech-loading pieces. (Reliable cast-iron cannon – an economical, but still less safe alternative to bronze – were first made in England and Sweden in the later sixteenth century.)

Cannon form also evolved. The fashion in the mid fifteenth century was for truly enormous stone throwers, the giant bombards. A few survivors still astound. 'Mons Meg', a Burgundian piece of 1449, has a bore of just under 50 centimetres, weighs 5,000 kilograms, and fired a shot of about 250 kilograms. The immense German mortar 'Pumhart von Steyr' tossed a ball of 80 centimetres diameter weighing almost 800 kilograms. This emphasis on the size of the projectile perhaps came from emulating the giant trebuchets; it was also a consequence of relatively weak and unreliable powder, which would have encouraged gunners to depend on the weight of the ball, as much as its velocity, to damage enemy walls. In the second half of the fifteenth century the monster bombards became curiosities. Experimentation pushed leaner forms, and armies tended to have more, smaller ordnance, though some pieces, especially for siege work, remained quite large.

Europe's gunmakers reached a consensus regarding form in the first decades of the sixteenth century: the smallest and specialized types aside, artillery should be muzzle-loading and cast of bronze in one piece; a gun should have a high ratio of length to bore (from about 12:1 to 40:1), and it should fire iron balls using corned powder. Ordnance came to be classed by proportion and size, with individual pieces rated by the weight of their projectile: full, half, and double cannon for close siege work, with longer-barrelled culverins of similar ball weights for more distant battery. (Culverins' longer barrels did not increase their range, but since bronze guns were cast breech-down in a pit, the metal at the breech of a culverin was under more pressure during casting than a shorter-barrelled cannon of similar bore; this made for a denser, stronger weapon more able to safely handle a larger charge of powder: a typical recommendation was to load a culverin with a charge of four-fifths the weight of the ball, and a cannon with a charge of only two-thirds the weight of the ball. Thus culverins really could shoot farther than cannon.) While essential to the siege, heavy cannons and culverins were awkward in the open field. Battlefield use was therefore mostly restricted to the quarter cannon, the lighter culverins, sakers, falcons and other types firing balls of roughly 12 to 15 pounds and under.

Sixteenth-century standardization included other design improvements. Trunnions, horizontally projecting lugs cast into the barrel at about the balancing point, allowed a weapon to be easily elevated and depressed with wedges. Carriages also markedly improved. A two-wheeled carriage with trail made a stable, triangular support for aiming, firing and recoil; attaching a two-wheeled limber quickly transformed this firing carriage into a flexible four-wheeled vehicle for hitching to teams of draught animals – multiple pairs of horses or oxen. Though bulky by the standards of later refinement, these carriages were an immense improvement over earlier platforms, sleds and four-wheeled carts, or the practice of wedging a naked barrel into the ground with stout timbers.

Against this overall pattern of design standardization, however, it must be acknowledged that surviving arsenal inventories often reveal cannon of surprisingly antique pattern, and manuals continued to discuss older types as if their readers would have real occasion to use them; thus, for example, a late-fifteenth-century long-barrelled passavolante (a precursor of the culverin) might easily have been used in defence of a place fifty or more years after its manufacture. Obsolescence is always relative to the needs of the moment. Speciality weapons also complicate the picture. The stumpy mortar, in some ways a survival of the bombard type, pitched an exploding bomb in a high arc to cross over a rampart and explode within a besieged town or citadel, burning houses and tormenting citizens. The organ gun, with

A woodcut of a military spectacular performed outside Munich by the Imperial Army of Charles V on 10 June 1530. Most of the cannon are large bronze pieces, with the exception of a single wrought-iron gun in the foreground, identifiable by its hooped barrel.

multiple small-calibre barrels mounted in a row on a single frame (hence the name), anticipated the modern machine-gun as a relatively rapid-firing anti-personnel weapon. And then there were the freaks: one beautifully crafted extant example, made for King Henry VIII of England in about 1533, is a cast-bronze triple-barrelled breech-loader. The ferocious ingenuity of the Renaissance arms manufacturer deserves note – European artisans clearly embraced gunpowder weapons with relish.

Europe's soldiers and soldier–rulers delighted in gunpowder, too. Traditionally historians have emphasized the distaste exhibited by the more old-fashioned, self-consciously chivalric members of the military aristocracy, men like the Italian condottiere Vitellozzo Vitelli (d. 1502, murdered by Cesare Borgia), who made a habit of chopping the offending limbs – their hands – from captured handgunners. Protesting about gunpowder was indeed commonplace. Authors equated it with the plague, and attached its invention to dark and sorcerous

TYPES OF RENAISSANCE ARTILLERY

Basilisks, serpents, minions, robinets, falcons, bastards, sirens, bases, slings: the multiple, evocative names of Renaissance artillery defy order, or even understanding – contemporaries railed against the needless proliferation of calibres, which could only complicate logistics and stymie wartime efficiency. Even after cannon came to be generally standardized by named category and weight of shot, the categories were not fully consistent between different services (say, Spanish and English) and measures differed between jurisdiction (as between Venetian and Milanese 'pounds' and 'feet'). But in the second half of the sixteenth century something like order came to Europe's arsenals, at least in theory. The following table approximates this consensus; it is based on figures in contemporary manuals (note that the distinction between a cannon and a culverin lay in the ratio of length to bore; culverins could be almost as heavy as cannon in weight of shot):

Type	Weight of ball	Weight of piece	Ratio of length to bore
Double cannon	100 pounds	20,000 pounds	20:1
Cannon	50	9,000	18:1
Half cannon	25	7,000	24:1
Quarter cannon	16	3,500	28:1
Culverin	25	2,000	36:1
Half culverin	15	1,700	40:1
Saker	6	2,500	32:1
Falcon	3	1,500	36:1
Falconet	1	500	40:1

CULVERIN
A line drawing of a small, wrought-iron culverin of the late fifteenth century.

experiment, even to the devil himself; and certainly the flash, billowing black smoke, and stink of sulphur all suggested hellfire. But despite this hint of damnation – which perhaps only added to the excitement – the more lasting mood was one of enthusiasm. Renaissance princes exulted in their guns (people still do), and they also enjoyed showing off their weapons. Gunfire thus entered the world of the political pageant. Army parades and drill demonstrations regularly included the firework-like discharge of small arms (with the occasional injury from a mistakenly loaded weapon). Though small explosions added a certain pop, they were nothing like the crash and boom of massed ordnance at a full military theatrical. At one such event, a 'triumph' – note the reference to an ancient emperor's display – held outside Munich in the summer of 1530 in honour of the newly crowned emperor Charles V, a small army put on a mock siege complete with mortars and cannon blasting away at a miniature fortress. And there was always the routine discharge of cannon salutes from citadels, warships and city walls to mark weddings and births, the arrival of important personages, notable saints' days and other ceremonial occasions. It was for moments like these that artillerists' manuals included recipes for gunpowder guaranteed to produce double the noise.

Princes thought of their cannon as pets, like great metal horses or dogs: it was no accident that certain types of gun (saker, falcon) were named after swift-killing hunting hawks. The most impressive cannon had given names: 'Great Devil', 'Queen', 'No More Words', 'Earthquake', even 'Bumblebee' (presumably from the buzzing of its missile in flight). They could have personal histories. The artillery-mad Duke Alfonso d'Este of Ferrara – his emblem a bursting bomb – boasted a park of over a hundred guns, including, among other exceptional pieces, the giant culverin 'Giulia' (Julia), wittily, if impiously, named after Alfonso's enemy Pope Julius II because it had actually been cast from the fragments of Michelangelo's statue of the Pope in Bologna, broken up and traded to Alfonso in 1511 after Julius lost control of the city. (The 158,000 pounds of bronze first intended for Leonardo da Vinci's

Ranges of Renaissance artillery

How far could a sixteenth-century cannon shoot? Contemporaries differed in their opinions – perhaps because their experience or sense of the problem differed. One answer comes from the Italian master gunner and engineer Eugenio Gentilini, who served in the armies of Venice, the grand duchy of Tuscany, and the knights of Malta. His 1598 *Instructions for Artillery* included a list of artillery ranges at both horizontal elevation ('*dritta linea*' or 'straight line') and, for maximum distance, at an elevation of 45 degrees. The term *dritta linea* was interchangeable with *punto bianco* (hence 'point-blank' in English), a reference to the ability of a gunner, when sighting along a level barrel, to see the white circle – the *punto bianco* or white point – at the dead centre of the practice target. Gentilini's figures are in 'natural walking paces' of two steps, or two and a half statutory feet each; remembering that the 'foot' varied by jurisdiction, a pace can be thought of as a little less than a modern English yard (0.91 metres).

Type	*dritta linea*	Extreme range
Musket	60 paces	1,200 paces
2-pound falconet	80	1,800
4-pound falcon	100	2,000
8-pound saker	150	2,500
14-pound culverin	200	3,500
16-pound 'canoncin'	150	2,500
20-pound cannon	180	2,800
20-pound culverin	250	3,800
30-pound cannon	200	3,000
30-pound culverin	260	4,000
40-pound cannon	220	3,000
40-pound culverin	300	4,000
50-pound cannon	250	3,500
50-pound culverin	300	4,000
60-pound cannon	250	3,500
60-pound culverin	300	4,000
90-pound cannon	250	3,500
90-pound culverin	300	4,000

100-pound cannon	250	3,500
100-pound culverin	300	4,000
120-pound cannon	250	3,500
120-pound culverin	300	4,000

Gentilini's contemporary Marc' Antonio Bellone supplied much more optimistic 'point-blank' and maximum ranges in his 1584 manual, *Instructions for Gunners*.

Type	Point-blank	Extreme range
Half cannon	500 paces	6,000 paces
Quarter cannon	450	5,400
Saker	350	4,200
Falcon	300	3,600
Falconet	250	3,000
Culverin	600	7,200
Half culverin	450	5,200

In service, gunners always tried to plant their weapons as close as possible; an Englishman in 1590 opined that 'for battery' pieces should be placed within 'eighty paces of their mark'. But long-distance sniping also took place. While holed up in the Castel' San Angelo during the Spanish sack of Rome in 1527, the goldsmith-turned-gunner Benvenuto Cellini used a falconet to clip a Spanish officer in two at such an extreme range that Pope Clement himself asked for an explanation of the trick shot. All in all, the effective range of a given gun of a given type varied greatly depending on the quality and condition of the gun and carriage, and of the powder used, whether the ball was truly round and of the proper calibre, how well the charge and ball were packed into the bore, and, finally, the skill of the gunner who aimed the piece. Sometimes the condition of the gunner mattered, too: at the siege of Oudenaarde in 1582 a drunken Spanish gunner fired directly into his own camp, interrupting the dinner party of the Spanish commander-in-chief, Alessandro of Parma, who, unhurt and nonplussed, continued with his meal even as his dead and dying companions were removed from table.

immense statue of Francesco Sforza in Milan had instead gone to make cannon for Duke Alfonso's father, Ercole d'Este.) Little guns were also fun, and nobles and kings were not above mechanical tinkering. Charles V messed with clocks and the clock-like mechanisms of early pistols, and the Scottish adventurer–assassin Robert Stuart, who claimed to be a relative of Mary, Queen of Scots, gained a reputation in France as a maker of extra strong armour-piercing bullets known as 'stuardes'. In Europe there was no meaningful cultural divide between the military technologist and the ruler. Men like Duke Alfonso d'Este and King Henry VIII, the emperor Charles V and Charles's grandfather the

THE HUNGRY GUNS

In a siege operation, maintaining a steady volume of fire was at least as important as its accuracy or range. Besieging batteries had to keep up a steady fall of shot on target walls and bastions to prevent the besieged from quickly rebuilding them, or preparing a second line of defences just to the rear. Gun crews laboured in rotation to load, aim, fire, sponge, scrape and reload with a minimum of interludes to let gun barrels cool. Metal, ceaselessly expanding and contracting, would eventually give way; sometimes only the muzzle of a piece flew off, broken away by an escaping ball; at other times the entire breech would rip, potentially maiming or killing dozens of men. Meanwhile the barrage had to be maintained, because a siege was always a kind of a race: between the besieging army and a potential relieving force; between the attacking cannon and the defending labourers; between the treasure available to prosecute a siege and the relentlessly mounting costs of maintaining a force in the field – wages, food, fodder, and the voracious appetite of the guns, especially for expensive gunpowder. The table below is from Girolamo Cataneo, *The Bombardier's Examination*, 1567.

Working from Cataneo's recommendation that a siege train appropriate 'for battery' should consist of no fewer than 2 culverins,

emperor Maximilian were both gunpowder warfare enthusiasts and powerful princes who both caused and directed wars; without this coincidence, without these princes' fascination with and commitment to an emerging new art of war, there could have been no military Renaissance.

An obvious ingenuity went towards the design of increasingly useful and stylish ordnance, but Renaissance military men devoted as much energy, and even more original thought, to the problems of resisting cannon, and the intriguing possibility of creating a novel system of military architecture that best took advantage of the new world of firepower. This justly celebrated exercise – the principles of Renaissance

3 full cannons, 4 half cannons, 8 quarter cannons (for which he fails to give the powder consumption), 8 falcons or sakers, and 12 falconets, this yields stupendous total figures for a day's gunfire: 3,410 shots fired, and 32,300 pounds of gunpowder consumed (and these figures leave out the 8 quarter cannon). The guns were also hungry for men to serve them. In 1595 the Venetian artillerist Ruscelli reflected that a 50-pound cannon needed 3 master bombardiers and 15 assistants; a 20-pound cannon 2 masters and 10 assistants; a 14-pound culverin 2 masters and 10 assistants; and a 12-pound saker 1 master and 5 assistants. Drovers and auxiliary craftsmen (carpenters, farriers, blacksmiths) numbered in the dozens; pioneers to labour at digging emplacements and building gabions were needed in the hundreds. Modern war did not come cheap.

Type	Shots per day	Pounds of powder per day
60-pound cannon	80	3,200
50-pound culverin	45	1,500
30-pound half cannon	110	2,200
6-pound saker or falcon	120	720
3-pound falconet	140	420

Moving artillery

Moving a 7-, 10-, or 20,000-pound siege cannon, or even a relatively small 1,000- or 2,000-pound field piece, required an enormous amount of human and animal muscle power, not only to drag along on campaign, but also to shift and aim once in battery. In his 1584 treatise *Instructions for Gunners*, Marc' Antonio Bellone offered as a rule of thumb the ratio of one pair of oxen or horses per 1,000 or 1,200 pounds of metal (ignoring the weight of the carriage). He also included a little table, noting that these figures were for dry, flat terrain; even more animals were needed on hills and when conditions turned muddy:

Type	Pairs of horses or oxen
Cannon of 10,000 pounds	10
Half cannon of 7,000 pounds	7
Quarter cannon of 3,500 pounds	4
Saker of 2,500 pounds	2
Falcon of 1,500 pounds	1
Double cannon of 20,000 pounds	20
Culverin of 15,000 pounds	15

The Spaniard Lechuaga gave similar numbers in his 1611 treatise, *On Artillery*. As was common, he advised carrying a heavy full cannon strapped to stout poles and suspended in a cradle so that its great weight would be divided between four large, sturdy wheels. Lifting these cannon from cradle to carriage and back with winch, tackle and tripod must have added considerably to the time, effort and risks of transportation. Lechuaga's figures:

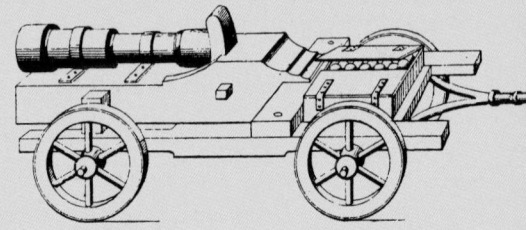

A wrought-iron field gun of the late fifteenth century, mounted on a carriage with an attached ammunition box. A piece this size needed only four to six draught animals.

Type	Draught horses
Full cannon in a cradle	21
Half cannon on carriage	15
Quarter cannon on carriage	9
Each empty cradle	9
Each covered wagon	9

Records from actual armies in the field confirm these numbers, and give staggering totals of draught animals. A relatively small Dutch train at Julich in 1610 needed 490 horses to pull 24 heavy wagons, 16 two-horse carts, and 15 artillery pieces (including only 2 full cannon): even more draught teams were needed for the 198 other wagons associated with the artillery (41 of which were for officers' baggage). Considering that a full siege train might easily consist of forty or more pieces, many of them full and half cannon, the necessary horses or oxen had to number in the thousands. Servicing these beasts took incredible effort. Daily fodder had to be found by the ton – which is why large-scale offensive operations were almost always limited to the grass-growing season, and why armies on the march cut a wide swathe of destruction across the countryside, as outriding foragers searched for animal feed. Unmetalled roads and weak bridges also complicated movement. In Piedmont in 1529 a retreating French army lost a cannon (as well as its master, crew and equipment) to pursuing Spaniards when a bridge collapsed beneath its weight and it could not be lifted from the mud. Such small disasters underlined the wisdom of secretly burying artillery pieces, hoping to recover them later, or breaking cannon into more portable pieces for future recasting, when an army needed to beat a quick retreat. Some transport problems could be avoided by travelling by river or, in northern Italy and the Netherlands, by canal; though often just as slow, fewer animals were needed to tow a boat or barge than in cross-country haulage. The difficulties of moving heavy guns inspired Renaissance mechanics to invent elaborate winch systems with multiple pulleys and gear trains. Giulio Savorgnano, chief engineer to the Venetian Republic at the end of the sixteenth century, had one winch so powerful that with it his pet dwarf Gradasso could single-handedly pull five artillery pieces (they must have moved very, very slowly).

fortification would shape the practice of war until the industrial revolution – was not an obvious or even a necessary development. More powerful artillery did not demand a different and better kind of fortress, only a stronger one. And the first sustained response to bombard and culverin, to the evolving powerful cannon types, was a brute strengthening of medieval traditions in military architecture. This was no new trend, either. European city and castle walls had been steadily growing more solid, more elaborate and more expensive for centuries: masonry had replaced earth and timber; great keeps, barbicans and concentric walls had replaced simpler plans; and the trebuchet had already served notice that tall, thin curtain walls would no longer suffice. So the obvious first solution to the added problems of gunpowder siegecraft – cannon, but also explosive mines – was to build metres-thick, immensely strong multi-storeyed stone towers. To fight fire with fire these towers mounted their own artillery, shooting through slits and slots from gunrooms deep within the stonework. There were problems with this approach. Besides a reverberating concussion at every discharge, these rooms must have quickly filled with noxious, slow-clearing fumes (some extant examples have chimneys and ventilation ports), and the size of a gunroom sharply limited the size of the cannon that could be accommodated. Bigger guns were better mounted at the open top of the tower, where a thick parapet with embrasures for return fire gave almost as much protection as an interior gunroom.

Artillery towers had other design weaknesses – flaws even, from the point of view of engineers searching out the perfect fortification design. An artillery tower was intended as a massive, self-defending strongpoint radiating defensive fire; to maximize that fire the tendency was to pile up the tiers of gunrooms. A surviving tower at Fougères in Brittany, built around 1480, has seven layers, including an open platform; the more typical south tower at Querfurth in Saxony, built by 1479, has four levels, three of them enclosed, plus the tower top. There is an interesting design parallel between these giant towers and the great bombards of a slightly earlier generation; both cannon makers and military architects clearly sought strength through size – but there were costs. In ordnance the giant bombards proved both slow-moving and slow-firing. In the case of the artillery tower, size made for easy targeting by attacking gunners. The obvious answer here was to mask a fortress with a wide and deep surrounding ditch; from a distance only the tower-tops would be visible and vulnerable to battery, but inside the ditch an assault party with ladders would still face dauntingly tall walls. But burying towers restricted the fire from guns mounted in lower, ditch-level gunrooms, and few sites allowed a perfect combination of truly deep ditch and tall interior wall: one that did was at Salses in Rousillon, where the Spanish, beginning in 1497, all but sank a massively reinforced castle into the landscape. Most fortresses had to accept a certain real exposure to enemy fire.

A graver problem with the artillery tower strongpoint concept was a potential vulnerability at its base. For centuries one of the primary goals of any besieging force was to lodge at the very bottom of a tower and undermine it. One technique was to replace removed stones with timbers and flammable refuse; when torched, the wooden supports burned away and the unbalanced tower toppled over. To prevent mining assaults such as these medieval castles and town walls developed elaborate vertical defences, overhanging wooden galleries (hoardings) and stone extensions (machicolation) with holes and hatches in the floor for dropping objects or firing directly down on mining parties. But hoardings and machicolation were exactly the sort of super-structure work that was most vulnerable to bombardment by cannon, or even trebuchet. And gunpowder added a new, spectacular dimension to the ancient techniques of mining assault. A gunpowder mine was used to blast over a tower at the Castilian siege of Moorish Malaga in 1487; and, more famously, the Spanish used a very large underground mine to explode and seize an entire outwork at their siege of the French-held Castello Nuovo in downtown Naples in 1495. In both cases, these early exploding mines seem to have demoralized already hard-pressed defenders, who soon surrendered.

The Castello Nuovo, Naples. Its story reflects the influence of gunpowder weapons on late medieval military architecture. First constructed in the late thirteenth century, the castle was rebuilt with larger, stouter towers between 1442 and 1451. In the 1460s a deeply scarped low wall was built at the level of the top of the moat to provide a firing platform for defending cannons. Finally, in the 1480s and 1490s, flanking positions were built at the bottom of the castle ditch.

How to prevent mining attack? Against sub-surface tunnelling the only possible response was counter-mining, which led to horrible underground combats with pistol, dagger and grenade. To defend against surface mining at the base of an artillery tower – since a vertical defence from above was now practically impossible – some kind of supporting, flanking fire was best. One solution was to place squads of infantry armed with handguns or very light artillery in small, pillbox-like outworks in front of an exposed tower; these positions would themselves be best protected if they were at the bottom of the fortress ditch. This is where the German artist Albrecht Dürer, in a 1527 treatise, placed casemates shaped like truncated cones to cover his proposal for a truly gigantic artillery tower. The Italian engineer Francesco di Giorgio, active in the late fifteenth century, sketched, among other varieties of small flanking works, spur-like casemates projecting from the base of a large tower. That in-close defence at the foot of a tower was not just a theoretical concern is shown, among other sites, by the surviving circular, pepper-pot-shaped casemates at the base of the massive Munot tower at Schaffhausen in Switzerland, built between 1563 and 1585.

An alternative to the masonry artillery tower was a more improvised defence based on earthworks and modifications to existing medieval walls and towers. This was a commonsense and effective, if sometimes inelegant, solution to the challenges of gunpowder warfare. At its most ad hoc, an improvised defence consisted of heaped-up earth, timber baulks, fascines (tied bundles of brush), gabions (giant wicker drums filled with earth) and even wool bales to block incoming shots; defending cannon would be emplaced where possible, and where they enjoyed a likely field of fire. In the sixteenth century improvising earthwork defences became a real craft and a serious part of a supervising engineer's job. He would first tour the perimeter of a threatened town to make his report, noting the vulnerabilities of old walls and towers and inadequate ditches. If a siege were at all likely the first order of business was clearing the suburbs of any houses, garden enclosures or other structures that might provide cover and ready-built positions for attacking artillery. This clearing had to be ruthless: gunpowder might be employed to quickly blow ancient churches and monasteries sky high (compensation-seeking lawsuits could stretch on for generations).

Next the existing defences had to be strengthened. Tall medieval gates and towers, their vertical defences now outmoded, had to be lowered to offer less of a target. Church towers inside the town would be spared. These were invaluable for observation, and also for mounting a few light pieces to snipe at the besiegers from a distance (during the siege of Florence in 1530 a defending gunner nicknamed 'the Wolf' pestered the Imperial Army from the heights of the St Miniato campanile, protected by 1,800 wool bales piled up or strapped to the tower). After all the preparatory demolition work the resulting rubble, together with fill from clearing and deepening the surrounding ditch, would be stacked behind the razed city walls to add protecting bulk. Next came the construction of raised artillery platforms, of two types: bastions projecting outside existing walls, and cavaliers built above existing walls or to their inside. The secret here was to minimize the number of strongpoints to maximize the concentration of defensive firepower, so bastions would first be planned for the high points and salient corners of the city perimeter, with others filling in so that all would be spaced the one from the next by roughly the distance of effective small arms fire, or point-blank artillery fire. Earthwork bastions and cavaliers were a ready and serviceable emulation of an artillery tower. Though they could not offer multiple tiers of gunnery, their earth and timber bulk could absorb considerable bombardment.

Earth platforms were not the only solution. A less well known earthwork-based defensive scheme, almost certainly originating in Germany, scattered small, circular infantry sconces in front of older medieval walls to provide a defence in depth – a very different concept from the artillery tower strongpoint. Each low sconce was completely surrounded by an earth palisade pierced with gunports; barbed-wire-like fence and palisade circuits helped impede any infantry assault. If infantry did advance within the belt of defending sconces they would be subject to withering, overlapping fire, while the men entrenched within each sconce would be invulnerable to the fire of their neighbours. This defence in depth technique, a fascinating anticipation of twentieth-century defensive tactics, was used by the imperial defenders at Pavia in 1525. Woodcuts show its use in central Europe through the 1530s. Later this specific defensive tradition seems to have merged with other, similar tactics based on chains of rectangular fortlets and angled connecting trench lines, tactics which remained an important part of the siege and siege-like field warfare so typical of the period through to the seventeenth century.

To build earthworks of any pattern required vast amounts of labour. Machiavelli, in his 1521 *Art of War*, advised that peasants made the

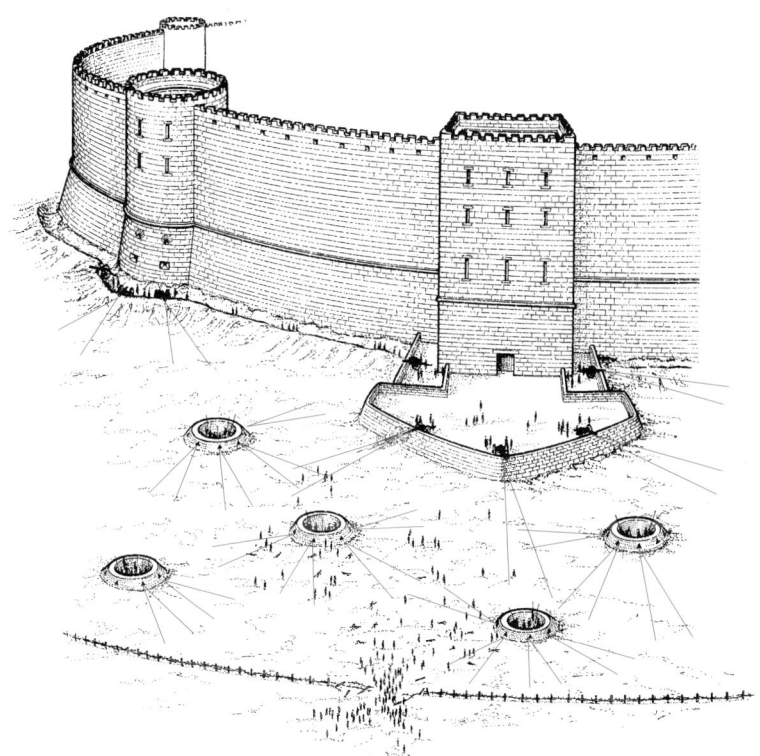

MUTUALLY SUPPORTING DEFENSIVE FIRE

One way of flanking a round artillery tower or other fortification was to provide an exterior defence in depth with a perimeter zone of earthwork sconces. This line drawing shows how lines of fire from mutually supporting sconces could destroy an attacking infantry force, while the defending arquebusiers and musketeers in each sconce would remain safe behind the protective walls of their own small earthwork.

best soldiers because their familiar peacetime work with spade and shovel was the duty most often required in the field. However, real soldiers often despised manual labour as inimical to their quasi-aristocratic martial ethos (many must have joined an army to escape such work), and they might refuse to dig even for extra pay. At the siege of the Castel Sant'Angelo in Rome in 1527 prisoners were forced to dig the besiegers' entrenchments. On the other side, citizens eager to save their skins and homes from the fury of a sack were often willing labourers on defensive works. Citizens were even more eager to pull down offending citadels which, unlike city walls, threatened rather than protected their liberty: at Siena in 1552 and at Antwerp in 1577, townspeople took advantage of lapses in Spanish authority to spontaneously assemble and tear down offending, overbearing bastions.

THE COST OF ARTILLERY

Though individual noblemen might have a personal small artillery piece or two, Renaissance war was indeed a sport of kings, or at least dukes: it took deep pockets to collect and maintain the big guns needed to defend or take a modern fortress. Naturally, the bigger the gun the more expensive. Ruscelli, in his 1595 manual *Precepts for a Modern Army*, included an exacting discussion of the costs of artillery (the figures below are rounded to the nearest ducat).

To put these costs in context, a single ducat would supply the daily wage for a common Venetian infantryman for about three months (about the same as an unskilled labourer). Experienced soldiers would receive a bit more. Helmet, breastplate and pike cost about three and a quarter ducats; an arquebus a little over one ducat.

Type	Cost of naked gun	Cost with carriage
120-pound cannon	1,269 ducats	1,310 ducats
100-pound culverin	1,227	1,069
80-pound cannon	781	814
50-pound culverin	781	812
50-pound cannon	472	501
20-pound culverin	314	334
20-pound cannon	177	294
12-pound saker	175	190
6-pound falcon	151	160
3-pound falconet	90	97

Detail from a Flemish tapestry, c. 1530, depicting the siege and battle of Pavia (1525).
At Pavia round sconces were built by German infantry defending the city against the
French. In this scene Swiss troops in French pay – including one woman camp
follower – are hastily evacuating a sconce captured from the defenders of the city in
earlier fighting. Similar round sconces were used to defend cities in Germany for ten
years or so after the battle of Pavia – after that the round sconces disappeared.

The most elegant solution to the problem of fortification in a gunpowder age emerged in Italy at around the turn of the sixteenth century: the angle bastion. At first glance, the angle bastion with its distinctive pointed salient appears to be just a quadrangular version of the artillery tower. But the theory behind the angle bastion was quite different: rather than radiating fire as a self-defending strongpoint, an angle bastion ultimately depended on the supporting fire of neighbouring angle bastions for its protection. Its secret feature lay in its side walls, the flanks. A pair or two of cannon mounted at each of these retired flanks were difficult to sight (and therefore target) by besieging gunners; however, though nearly hidden, these same pieces were perfectly sited for defensive fire, since their lines of fire exactly paralleled the face of the bastion opposite, ensuring that a single discharge would instantly decimate any infantry assault against that bastion. Also there was no place of safety for attackers to lodge and slowly sap an angle bastion, since the lines of flanking fire from adjacent bastions met and crossed at the salient point of the bastion they protected. This last technical point was a critical advantage over the round artillery tower, where an unavoidable dead zone at the base of the tower could only be flanked by potentially vulnerable exterior casemates (as in Dürer's 1527 treatise proposal). Of course, the top platform of an angle bastion mounted additional artillery that could reach out into the surrounding countryside, and the whole had to be protected by a deep ditch too.

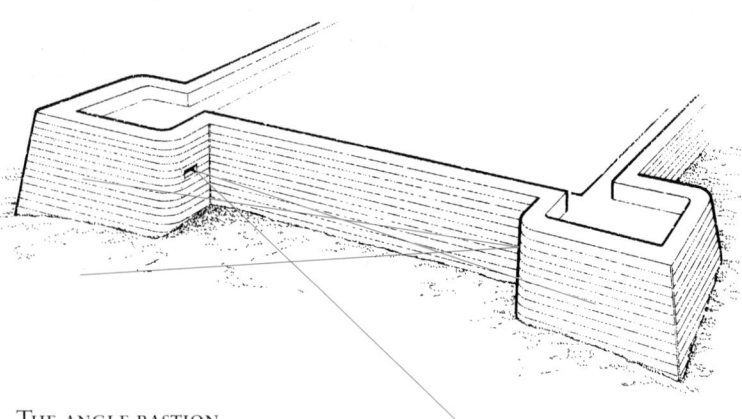

THE ANGLE BASTION

The secret of the angle bastion: artillery positions at the retired flanks of a pointed bastion can sweep the face of the bastion opposite, and since the lines of fire from two neighbouring bastions' flanks cross and meet at the point of every bastion, there is no place for an attacking mining party or infantry assault to shelter. The wide platforms at the top of each bastion provide further artillery positions. In the end the angle bastion concept proved the most attractive to Renaissance engineers and military architects – but it took time for the angle bastion system to win out.

The concept of the angle bastion, and the underlying idea of analysing a fortress plan as a Euclidean problem of lines of fire and lines of sight, was already under speculation in Italy by the mid fifteenth century (and in a practical way flanking fire had been used for centuries, but without intellectual explication). By the turn of the century the project of maximizing converging lines of fire had become a fascinating, almost obsessive intellectual game among Italian engineers and architects. Leonardo da Vinci, like his contemporaries, worked out multiple schemes for a perfectly flanked fortress. His sketches include designs for a massive deep wall, saw-toothed in plan, with a gunroom at every re-entrant angle; also a plan for an immensely tall artillery tower (for the Castello Sforzesco at Milan) which could vertically flank outer fortress walls with downward-slanting lines of fire. Leonardo's arch-rival Michelangelo similarly experimented, designing weirdly lobe-shaped bastions (some perhaps actually constructed in preparation for the 1530 siege of Florence) strangely sculpted by the requirements of many criss-crossing lines of fire. These designs, and others of the moment, are evidence that the angle bastion system was still in development. For example, like his contemporary Dürer in Germany, da Vinci fully explored the artillery tower, proposing a whole super-fortress of gentle curves and rounded parapets, the complete theoretical opposite to an angle bastion design.

While theorists tinkered towards perfection, actual angle bastions appeared. Perhaps their first true application in stone was at the papal fortress of Nettuno in 1501; embryonic bastions are visible in very late fifteenth-century projects at Sarzanello and Ostia, also along the western coast of Italy. (In truth the first real experiments were probably executed as less costly earthworks, perhaps even a generation earlier.) By the 1530s the angle bastion was the dominant, if not yet quite the exclusive, military architectural form in Italy; over the following twenty years Italian architects spread the new system of fortification to princely clients in Germany, France, Spain and England. Also in the mid century the Portuguese began refortifying their far-flung colonial

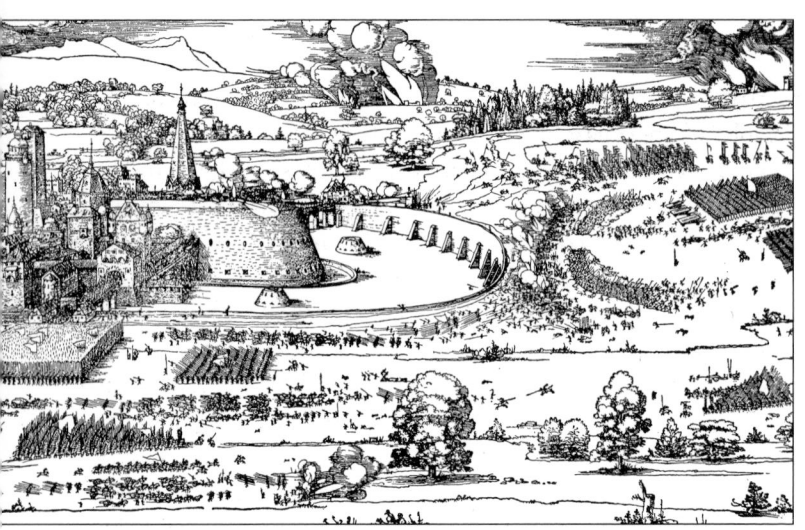

This woodcut by Albrecht Dürer is an illustration from his 1527 treatise proposing a truly massive artillery tower, as shown. To protect and flank that huge structure, Dürer here provides an enormous ditch with two large casemates, each an artillery tower in its own right. Artillery towers almost as large were actually built in Germany.

empire with new-style angle bastion defences. The first two published treatises to discuss the angle bastion system – with elaborate diagrams – appeared simultaneously in 1554: the confidential, proprietorial knowledge of the best Italian engineers was now public. An English manuscript translation of one of these treatises headed each page with the words 'the key of the Treasury'; in England at least this knowledge was still powerful, semi-secret stuff. By the end of the sixteenth century only Europe's wild, wild East – Poland and Russia – still built fortifications in the medieval manner. In the last third of the sixteenth century, whole major cities were belted anew with a perfectly geometrical perimeter of angle bastions; among the first grand plans was Nicosia in Cyprus, rebuilt by Venice from 1567.

Even more important than the actual, built monuments of angle bastion fortification was the fact that the general principle of maximizing flanking, enfilading fire entered other areas of the military art, particularly infantry tactics. The sensibilities as well as the principles of angle bastion architectural design found a home in the military mind: precision and repetition; an emphasis on form, on the shape of things; a habit of planning on paper, with diagrams; an affinity for rule and a confidence in theory. It was the spread of these sensibilities more than any new weapon or tactic (artillery, mines, angle bastions) that lay at the heart of an ongoing military Renaissance.

Which fortification system really worked best: elegant angle bastion, blunt artillery tower, earthwork platforms, or other schemes such as extended belts of casemates and sconces? Sixteenth-century military men overwhelmingly concluded that the angle bastion was the one true formula. A wave of competing but complementary treatises, some written by practised experts, others by cranks, exploded with variations on the angle bastion theme. These all provided exacting instructions for the construction of perfect bastions, including exact lengths for face and flank, and the precise angles of degree for salient and re-entrant. Real-world engineers followed these recipes, marking out the lines of bastion and curtain wall with cords and pegs, a textbook diagram brought to life. But there is little evidence that the age's lovingly crafted citadels and city wall systems were actually truly superior in wartime (there was no doubt they were superior in the imagination). Circumstances – the mood of the garrison, governor and citizens; the state of the storehouse and powder vault; the vagaries of weather and politics – made a mockery of theoretical perfection. The absolutely up-to-date, beautifully bastioned Venetian fortress-city of Nicosia fell to the Turks in 1570 after only seven weeks' resistance; during the same Cyprus war, the artillery towers and improvised earth platforms at Famagusta fanatically held out for eleven months, surrendering on terms (its governor was skinned alive for his temerity). In an interesting and almost solitary admission, in 1587 the experienced Huguenot captain François la Noue asserted, in the fourth of his military 'Paradoxes' (polished little essays on technical military problems), that in fact improvised fortifications of earth were 'no less

Renaissance fortifications

Renaissance princes and states invested enormous sums in the new military architecture, whether based on the artillery tower or the angle bastion. These two maps provide examples that demonstrate the spread of this new military architecture both in Europe and in the Spanish and Portuguese overseas empires. Two trends are visible: first, the concentration of effort in the areas of greatest conflict, including the frontier between Christendom and Islam; and second, the outward spread of the angle bastion system from Italy.

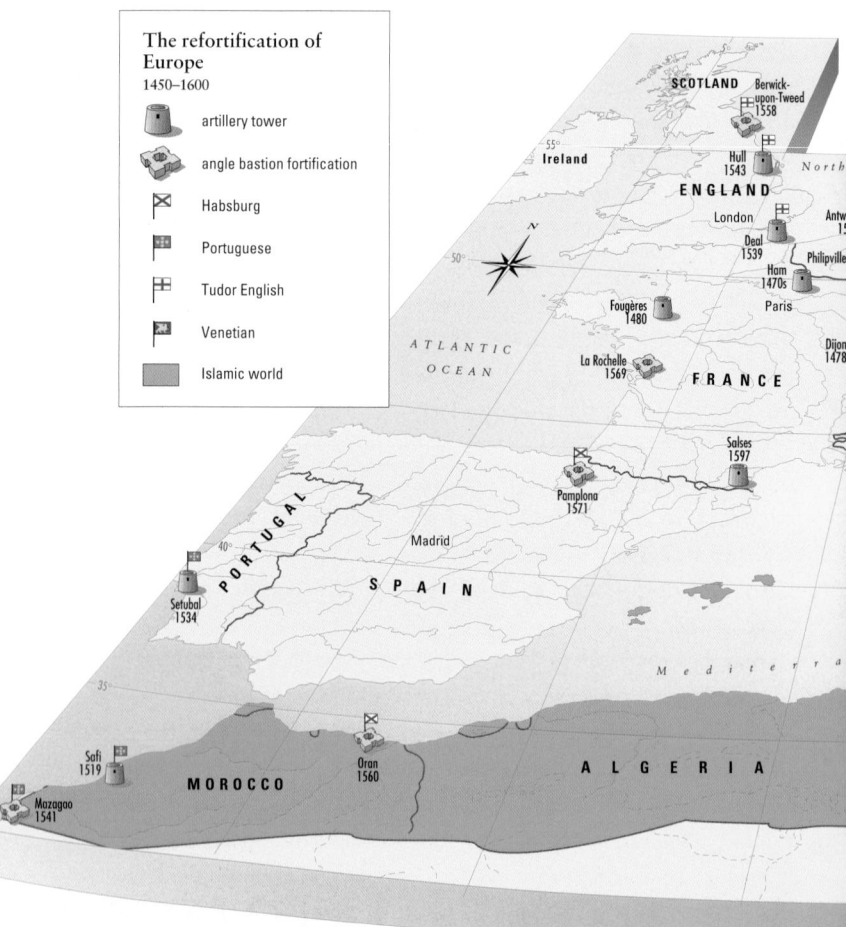

The refortification of
Europe
1450–1600

artillery tower

angle bastion fortification

Habsburg

Portuguese

Tudor English

Venetian

Islamic world

Fortresses of the world
1500–1600

Spanish trading routes

Portuguese trading routes

artillery tower

angle bastion fortification

Habsburg

Portuguese

Spanish base

Portuguese base

Spanish possessions

Portuguese possessions

165° 150° 135° 120° 105° 90° 75° 60° 45° 30° 15° 0° 15° 30° 45° 60° 75° 90°120° 135° 150° 165° 180° 165°

Arctic Circle

70°
60°
40°
Tropic of Cancer
10°
10°
20° Tropic of Capricorn
30°
40°
50°

PORTUGAL

SPAIN

Cuba
1511–33
Havana
Ponta Delgada
(Azores)
1551
Hispaniola
1492
Funchal
(Madeira)
1542
Canary Is.
Cape
Verde
Is.
São Tomé
1483
Diu
1546
Macao
1555
Nagasaki
1570
Formosa
Hormuz
1558
Malacca
1511
Manila
to Acapulco
Acapulco
Philippine Is.
Cartagena
Puerto Rico
1565
Lima
1535
Natal
1603
Rio de Janeiro
1565
Luanda
1576
Mombasa
1557
Goa
1510
Cochin
1503
Sumatra
Borneo
New Guinea
Ternate
1522
Java
Madagascar
Manila
Valparaíso
1536
Buenos Aires
1536
Safala
1505

UNITED
PROVINCES
Spandau
1578
Warsaw
POLAND
HOLY ROMAN EMPIRE
Rothenburg
1572
Vienna
1548
Kraków
1498
Schaffhausen
1563
Palmanova
1593
Karlstadt
1578
Buda
Pest
s Confederation
Venice
OTTOMAN
EMPIRE
EDMONT
Turin
1564
Pisa
1509
Florence
1534
Assisi
1535
Papal
States
Rome
Barletta
1527
Ragusa
1463
Corsica
Nettuno
1501
Naples
NAPLES
Brindisi
1538
Corfu
1530s
Modon
1490s
ardinia
Goletta
1535
Palermo
1535
Sicily
Messina
1535
s
Sea
TUNIS
Malta
1551
Nicosia
1567
Cyprus

inset not
to scale

defensible' than an expensive stone citadel designed by the priciest imported Italian engineer. Of course, imagination and reality do overlap: governments knew that modern bastioned walls signalled a military and political vitality; they announced that this was a state that had to be reckoned with. Thus even the seemingly insignificant lesser territorial rulers of Italy and Germany – minor princes, free cities and ecclesiastics – embraced the expensive new architecture as wholeheartedly as the great monarchs and republics. In the end, even as the angle bastion itself spread across the landscape of Europe it was the idea or spirit of the angle bastion that most thoroughly penetrated Europe's war-making community.

As the art of making a fortress became more regular, more confident and more sophisticated – even scientific – so the art of taking a fortress had to respond. Siegecraft acquired a whole new intensity and discipline, particularly in the case of an important town – and increasingly the siege of such a place came to be the whole point of a year's campaign. First the city under attack had to be sealed from outside communication, as far as possible, with a continuous circuit of infantry camps, cavalry patrols and guard posts. By the end of the sixteenth century this circuit would usually be a continuous belt of sconces and trenches. If there was a risk of a relieving army approaching then a second, outward-facing line of defences was also necessary. The attacking general and his staff of engineers and captains, if they had not already done so, next had to choose a focus for their attack, their point of concentration: an ill-sited bastion, an older stretch of curtain, a decayed gate tower. Then the slow-moving great guns, the essential tools of siege warfare, had to be strained into position and emplaced with protecting earthworks and gabions. Height was an advantage here: to overlook your target meant everything. The besiegers – or, more likely, the impressed peasantry of the surrounding country – might build great platforms, cavaliers, to raise up the attacking guns. At Haarlem in 1573 the Spanish besiegers erected musket-proof wooden cages on tall poles for snipers to fire into the defenders' works.

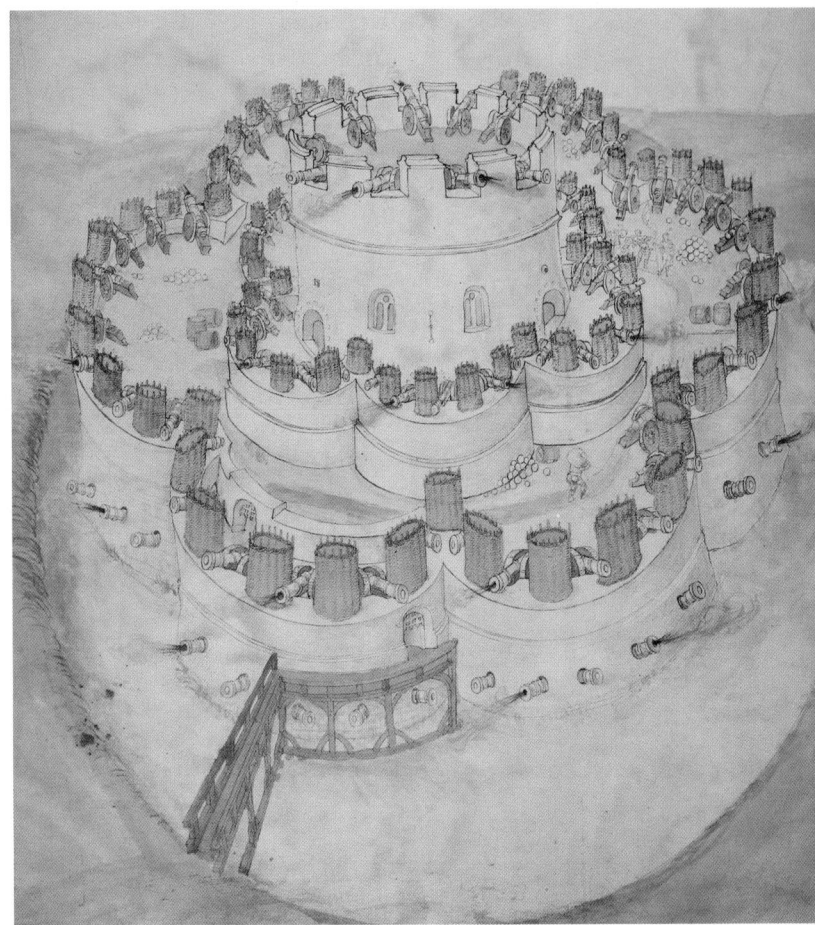

A drawing of an artillery fortress for the south coast of England in the late 1530s. At this date the secrets of the angle bastion were still unknown and unappreciated in northern Europe; Henry VIII's forts along the English channel were large and elaborate artillery towers. In this proposal the guns at platform level are protected by gabions, wickerwork barrels filled with earth. Though not designed in the most fashionable manner – by the standards of the most sophisticated continental engineers – a fortress of this scale and firepower (though the number of defending cannon is certainly exaggerated) would still be a tough nut to crack.

WAGONS AND BARRELS, HORSESHOES AND SHOVELS

The equipment for a full artillery train in the field consisted of much more than guns, carriages and a few wagons of shot and powder: the necessary materials and hardware for clearing the route of march, constructing emplacements and keeping everything in good repair made up an impressive catalogue; no doubt a daunting one for the responsible master of artillery, considering that the lack of any one thing – say, a tow rope or a hammer – might, like the proverbial horseshoe nail, jeopardize a day's march or a week's bombardment. Therefore capable masters kept careful, up-to-date lists, making the enterprise of managing artillery on campaign, particularly during an extended siege, as much a business of accounting as anything else. Below are selected entries from a detailed list itemizing the artillery train of Emperor Charles V during the 1546–7 Schmalkaldic War in Germany:

Item	Amount
Full cannons	10
Half cannons	12
Culverins	4
Half culverins	17
Sakers	7
Falcons	16
Half falcons (falconets?)	2
Balls for full cannons	3,993
Balls recovered from those fired by the enemy at Ingolstadt	568
Balls for half cannons	4,243
Balls for culverins	380
Balls for half culverins	2,154
Balls for sakers	1,768
Balls for half sakers	360
Balls for falcons	2,350
Cannon powder	2,759 quintals
Arquebus powder	1,000 quintals
Saltpetre	396 pounds
Sulphur	650 pounds

Item	Amount
Charcoal	2 cartloads
Matchcord	286 quintals
Lead	975 quintals
Tripod frames for lifting cannon	3
Tents and pavilions	23
Barrels	185
Iron bolts with nuts	500
Iron nails	150 gross
Raw iron for working	28,015 pounds
Hammers	8
Pincers	34
Bellows	10
Stoves	4
Grapples	3
Crowbars	22
Wooden trunks	38
Turpentine	1 barrel
Cash strongboxes	2
Lanterns	50
Wicker baskets	600
Hemp tow ropes for horses	490
Sickles for cutting fascines	750
Shovels	4,871
Axes for cutting wood	510
Pickaxes	2,762
Spades	5,561
Spare tool handles	600
Scythes to cut grass for forage	150
Small sickles	700
Horseshoes	3,600
Horseshoe nails	150,000

Once the barrage began it had to be steady, ideally furious. Each type of gun had its role: the great cannons and culverins to blast away at rampart and tower; the lesser artillery and infantry fire to keep the defenders' heads down and harass the work of repair; the mortars to extend destruction into the town. Artistry here mixed with brutality. In a well-directed operation co-ordinated attacking lines of fire reached out to destroy, one by one, the most critical defensive positions. The first priority was the defending guns, particularly at the bastion flanks; once the defenders' fire slackened the besieging artillery could be re-emplaced at a hundred paces' range or less. It was then the real pounding commenced, and sooner or later even the stoutest wall would fail, opening up a breach for the besiegers to assault – they

The storming of Parma in 1521, a painting by Tintoretto, c. 1580. Though imprecise this magnificent painting gives an excellent sense of the energy and emotion of a great assault operation. Such an attack was easily among the most psychologically daunting battlefield circumstances a Renaissance soldier could face – it was not unheard of for otherwise brave troops to refuse an assault on a breach they regarded as simply too dangerous to attempt.

hoped it would be a wide breach, with a gentle forward slope of rubble filling the ditch. Now came the infantry assault, with ladders and banners and beating drums. The psychology of this moment for the attackers must have been especially intense; after all, there was always the possibility of a horrible massacre along ditch and rampart: a single well-placed cannon loaded with nails and stones or small shot could devastate a mass of men crammed in a breach. A clever defence could make the breach dangerous in other ways. At the siege of Padua in 1509 the Venetian defenders mined their own bastions; when one was taken, the mine was set off, blasting the attackers to smithereens. Secondary, interior fortifications could also be built to enclose and enflank a breach from the rear, making it a cul-de-sac beaten with crossfire. If attacking troops did carry the breach, and did break through to the town beyond, the massacre would be among the garrison and unlucky civilians; custom allowed a three-day sack for the troops to vent their fury. A timely surrender could prevent this final tragedy.

But not all sieges concluded in surrender or sack; they remained uncertain affairs. They were, above all, exhaustive in nature: expensive in time, treasure and troops. The mortality of an assault could be dreadful, but it was daily life in camps and trenches that really drained an army, the constant drip of desertion and death by disease. Against a professionally prepared and vigorously defended city a siege operation was a major gamble, the commitment of a good-sized army for many weeks and even months.

There were alternatives to the full-blown siege. As fortifications became more difficult to reduce without costly and time-consuming battery, attackers sought to exploit every possible weakness: gates were an obvious vulnerability. Commando tactics appeared. One technique depended on the petard, a bell-shaped bronze or iron pot packed with gunpowder. In a lightning raid the intrepid petardier – a well rewarded volunteer (should he live) – nailed or wedged his instrument against a city or fortress gate, lit the fuse and ran.

Sometimes he didn't get far enough away before the bomb blew – hence Shakespeare's phrase 'hoist with his own petard'. After the petard opened the way an assault party would rush in – with luck before the watch could rally the defenders. In their first spectacular demonstration Henry of Navarre used petards to blast through outer and inner gates and seize the town of Cahors in 1580. A more stealthy technique was to use screwjacks or giant wrenches to quietly break apart the iron grates protecting sewer outlets. The *ruse de guerre* was another risky but highly cost-effective siege alternative. Many of these were variations on the Trojan Horse. In 1590 eighty Dutch soldiers infiltrated and then seized the city of Breda by hiding at the bottom of a ferry boat. Seven years later Spanish soldiers dressed as peasants took Amiens by simply walking up to the open gate, stalling a wagon in the gateway to prevent the gate or portcullis from closing, and overpowering the guard. To discover such tricks guards at city gates were supposed to use their halberds to probe wagonloads of hay and other likely hiding spots.

At the opposite end of the general's repertoire there was the slowest but surest siege method of all: blockade. A large city needed a steady supply of victuals from the countryside; stockpiles could last only so long. Controlling food consumption then became key. In 1567 the Huguenots blockading Paris burned the suburban windmills (needed to grind grain for flour) to increase pressure on the town. Inside a city under siege, municipal authorities often broke or confiscated distillery equipment to make sure that precious grain was used for bread, not wasted to make liquor. Authorities also drew up lists of essential and not-so-essential citizens; only the former got tickets for bread, and the latter were expelled from the city as 'useless mouths'. Besiegers often refused to let these unfortunates pass through the siege lines; the starving creatures would end up trapped between besieger and besieged, pitifully pleading for relief. As always in time of war, it was the poor and the weak who suffered first and suffered the most.

CHAPTER TWO

The New Legions

A scene from the battle of Pavia (1525), a detail from a series of seven tapestries manufactured in the Brussels workshop of Barnaert van Orley, c. 1530. The tapestries were made for the Marquis of Pescara, an important Imperial commander at the battle. In this scene mounted French men-at-arms charge across the foreground; the central figure is King Francis I, identifiable by the lilies of France on the chest of his horse. To the rear stands a body of Imperial arquebusiers.

The New Legions

ON 24 JULY 1534 King Francis I of France issued a remarkably bold ordinance formally reorganizing the infantry of his kingdom along explicitly antique lines: seven 'legions' of 6,000 men each – the figure was plucked directly from ancient Roman sources – were to be raised from the native sons of seven different regions (Burgundy, Champagne, Guyenne, Languedoc, Normandy, Picardy, and Dauphiné and Provence combined). It was an ambitious and novel military reform, entirely without precedent in France. Officers were to come from the regional nobility who, in return for their willingness to march on foot at the head of a legion, would be excused both certain taxes and their ancestral feudal obligation of serving the king as armoured knights on horseback. At least for those gentry who accepted a position in a legion – and of course Francis hoped they would – a traditional, medieval way of war based on lances and horses was to be replaced by a modern military ethos based on ranks and files of foot soldiers marching in step; in fact, marching like ancient Romans. Francis's legionary reform scheme was thus as much cultural as technical or tactical. It was a conscious attempt to create not only a useful and disciplined infantry for the king, but to place the peculiar experience of ordered, disciplined infantry service – the rhythm of the drill square, in short – at the heart of the art of war in France.

Though unprecedented, the boldness of Francis's new legions project was entirely in character with the times. During the same summer of 1534 Jacques Cartier discovered the St Lawrence river, France's first great moment of overseas discovery; and in October clandestinely posted Protestant broadsides denouncing the Catholic mass appeared in the streets of Paris, the first sign of a French religious crisis that would all but destroy the country before the century was out. In the mid 1530s, Renaissance France bubbled with experiment and reform.

King Francis's difficult military and political situation also encouraged a bold experiment. On the one hand, by the 1530s there

Two ordered battalions, each a square of pikemen with a flanking sleeve of arquebusiers: a detail from a woodcut showing a review of Emperor Charles V's army outside Munich on 10 June 1530. These men had just marched north from the wars of Italy, where the new disciplined infantry tactics were first created. Note the pair of multi-barrelled organ guns to the right flank of the infantry squares – exactly where we would expect infantry support artillery to be placed.

was a real sense of exhaustion and exasperation at the prospect of paying through the nose, as French monarchs had been doing for decades, for Swiss mercenary infantry: ferocious soldiers, but expensive and notoriously impudent, as famous for their cranky independence as for their battlefield courage. Manufacturing their more tractable replacement (as had already been done elsewhere) seemed a laudable goal. Also Francis still burned from his humiliating capture at the disaster of Pavia (1525) and subsequent imprisonment in Madrid under the very thumb of his arch-rival, Emperor Charles V. To match and defeat the emperor's vaunted Spanish and German infantry, the best in Europe, Francis desperately needed a core force of modern, disciplined, loyal foot. Revenge required nothing less.

An army in the field

Renaissance armies varied widely in size and composition. Probably the most representative of progressive practice was that maintained in the Netherlands by King Philip II of Spain to suppress the Dutch Revolt. This was a large and polyglot force, raised from every corner of the Spanish Habsburg Empire – and beyond. Under the command of the Duke of Alva (1567–73) and then the Duke of Parma (1578–92) the reputation of this force was second to none. Below is the official, if largely theoretical, strength for the Spanish Army in the Netherlands, dated 18 December 1573. These troops were scattered in winter quarters throughout the loyal Netherlands.

Unit	Companies	Men
Infantry		
Tercio (regiment) of Naples	19	1,900
Tercio of Lombardy	10	1,000
Tercio of Sicily	15	1,500
Tercio of Flanders	10	1,000
Tercio of Lombardy, presently in Italy	25	2,500
German infantry at 300 men per company	86	25,800
Walloon infantry at 200 men per company	104	20,800
Total	269	54,500
Cavalry		
Scouts armed with light arquebuses	1	300
Men-at-arms	15	3,000
Spanish, Italian and Albanian light cavalry	14	980
Mounted arquebusiers at 100 men per company	5	500
Total	35	4,780

But why reach back to long-gone days – why resurrect the Roman legion, a military system dead for over a thousand years? Because Francis and his military advisers assumed, as a basic principle of their Renaissance culture, that Rome and Greece still provided excellent – indeed, the best – models for improving present-day life: in architecture, in literature, and so also in warfare. To reform the infantry of France on the model of the legion was no more odd than building a church in the image of an ancient pagan temple. What we in our own time would consider a hopelessly anachronistic gesture – reaching back to ancient Rome for a practical reform agenda – was, in 1534, a sensible and progressive act of policy.

There were problems, of course, in making Francis's utopian *ordonnance* a reality. Recruits were not easily or instantly transformed into disciplined legionaries straight from the pages of Livy, and reasons of cost (there are always reasons of cost) limited the experiment to four legions, not seven. But despite shortcomings and compromises the 1534 reform for the first time provided the kings of France with an ordered and loyal native French infantry, and the four legions actually raised continued in name into the tumultuous Religious Wars of the second half of the century. Thereafter the surviving legions evolved to become the original line regiments of the *ancien régime*; they were the progenitors of a proud institution, *l'armée de France*, that exists to the present day. In actual practice the newfangled French legions of the mid 1530s and after seem to have formed and drilled much like any other well-ordered European infantry of their day. Overt references to the original ancient model – terminology, formations – mostly disappeared. But the underlying, more fundamental connection with the idea of the Roman legion remained: the idea of a disciplined and formally drilled infantry, ideally raised from native subjects and officered by a native military aristocracy. It is this greater and more general fidelity to the ancient example that is the real point, since much of the organizational and tactical innovation that transformed European infantry practice over the wider sixteenth century – the phrase infantry revolution would not be too strong – was driven by the same widespread fascination with the armies of Caesar and Alexander that inspired Francis I. Throughout the sixteenth century experienced, sophisticated military men – not just bookish theorists – seriously laboured to recreate, both on paper and on the drill field, the regular forms and regular discipline of the infantry armies of the ancient world.

Among the most famous of these truly Renaissance-minded reformers were the Nassau cousins, Protestant noblemen and professional generals at the end of the sixteenth century. In December 1594 William Louis of Nassau dreamed up a new musketry fire discipline after reading a description by the ancient author Aelian of Roman soldiers discharging flights of javelins and sling-stones. William Louis immediately included a description of his brainwave in a letter to his cousin Maurice of Nassau, commander-in-chief of the Dutch States forces fighting against Habsburg Spain. Maurice took his cousin's suggestions seriously, and another Nassau cousin, William Louis's brother John, made them an essential part of a successful new regulation drill for the Dutch Army. There were others in the Dutch camp mining Roman warfare for policy advice. Maurice was also influenced by the humanist 'Justus Lipsius', author of a 1595 analysis of the Roman Army. The antique origin of the Nassau brothers' reforms was recognized and celebrated by contemporaries. In 1616 the Dutch infantry drill was put into English as *The Tactics of Aelian*, a book which approvingly compared and connected

ancient and modern infantry techniques. Others were at work on the same reconciliation. Even as the Nassau cousins were experimenting with ancient drills in the north, in Italy Francesco Patrizi was preparing and publishing (1595) his *Military Parallels*, a book dedicated to the

An engraving from Leonhard Fronsperger's 1565 treatise, the Book of War, *of an ideal army encampment. Inspired by the legionary camps in ancient Roman texts, Renaissance reformers proposed strictly ordered camps to encourage and enforce an army's overall discipline.*

project of accommodating 'the various customs and the regulations of the ancients' to modern firearms: the 'parallels' of Patrizi's title were those that connected Roman and modern infantry disciplines – very satisfying stuff to the Renaissance mind. Patrizi's goal, interestingly, was to help European infantry counter the superior numbers of the Ottoman sultan (1595 was a war year between Turk and emperor in Hungary). As in the north, in Italy experiment was actual as well as mental. In his book Patrizi mentions one Antonio Giorgio Besozzi, a captain for the Duke of Savoy in the 1580s, as having 'formed a militia according to the rules of the ancients'. Francis I's legions project of 1534 was thus one of the first of many serious, high level military reforms based on ancient models.

Perhaps the first sustained effort of an infantry reform *all'antica* – 'after the antique' – was that promoted by Bartolomeo d'Alviano in 1513–14 for the armies of the republic of Venice. (Four years previously, Venice had suffered her worst land defeat of the century at the battle of Agnadello; as in France after Pavia, in Venice a particularly bold reform seems to have followed in the wake of a particularly hard disaster.) Alviano proposed regular and standard infantry companies of 256 men, a perfect square formation of sixteen ranks and sixteen files. Organizational details confirm Alviano's commitment to ancient forms and language: each sixteen-man file was to be a separate sub-unit, a 'decuria' led by a 'decurione' and closed by a 'tergiductor' – these Latinate titles and roles were directly borrowed from surviving ancient drills. Alviano's infantry project can be compared with a 1529–30 Venetian naval experiment, directed by the classicist Vettor Fausto, to scrupulously reconstruct an immense Roman galley, a quinquereme. Again, military experiment after the antique was a recognized problem-solving technique, not a flight of folly. (Over the next fifteen years, France, Spanish-allied Genoa and even the Ottoman sultan all built their own experimental galleys *all'antica*.) As in so many other areas of Renaissance life and thought, looking to the deep past opened up the possibility of present-day change.

It is important to remember that the infantry reformers who looked to the ancient example were searching for an overall improvement in discipline and control, not just tactical tricks. In the Renaissance world the culture of infantry soldiering was essentially mercenary. Most companies were raised and led by noble captain–entrepreneurs who might – or might not – be fighting for their legally rightful lord. The rank and file hardly cared for whom or for what they were fighting, as long as they were paid: thousands of Christian renegades happily served Muslim princes in the Eastern Mediterranean and North Africa. Coin was king. In some circumstances (such as Spanish service), and particularly among the emerging noble-born officer corps, something like a patriotic sense of duty was evolving, but these sentiments were far from universal. A seasoned unit could be professionally skilled, with the *esprit de corps* of a band of brothers, and still be far from easily led or managed.

Financial problems exacerbated every difficulty, and governments – which were usually mortgaged to the hilt – tended to form and hire armies larger than their capacity to sustain in the field. As a result negotiation and argument between masters and hired hands over missed pay musters, suspicious unit tallies and the like were a tedious constant of campaign life. Mutinies were not only common, but could be spectacular: in 1576 aggrieved Habsburg troops, led by a strike leadership elected from the ranks, sacked the city of Antwerp in what became known as the 'Spanish Fury' – some of the mutinous infantry units had not been paid in four years. Given these problems of mercenary culture and perilous finances, how could the will of the individual soldier be better connected with the will of the state? Here the legions of Rome, particularly Republican Rome, seemed the perfect model. Though most Renaissance rulers and governments accepted various degrees of mercenary custom as the ruling system, some intellectuals and humanistically educated generals dreamed of recovering what they imagined were the linked military virtues of ancient Rome: tactical perfection, absolute steadfastness in battle and devotion to the state. Roman martial virtue, at once technical and political, was especially

THE COST OF INFANTRY

'No silver, no Swiss', pithily observed the Italian captain Trivulzio early in the sixteenth century. Many others, doubtless with an inward sigh, paraphrased the ancient maxim: 'coin is the sinew of war'. The costs indeed were great. Below are the monthly expenses for a Spanish tercio of twenty-four companies serving in the Netherlands under the Duke of Alva in the early 1570s.

Item	Monthly cost in ducats
2 colonels at 80 ducats each	160
16 halberdier guards at 4 ducats each	64
22 captains at 40 ducats each	880
24 lieutenants at 12 ducats each	288
24 sergeants at 5 ducats each	120
200 corporals at 3 ducats each	600
48 drummers at 3 ducats each	144
24 fifers at 3 ducats each	72
4,000 pikemen at 3 ducats each	12,000
1,000 arquebusiers at 4 ducats each	4,000
360 musketeers at 3 ducats each	1,080
Expenses at 50 ducats per company	1,200
Scribe, doctors, surgeons and other officials	252
Total	20,860

attractive to those men charged with ordering the military affairs of the surviving great Italian republics, Venice and Florence, where the Roman Republican example felt particularly appropriate. In early sixteenth-century Venice, along with his tactical reforms, Bartolomeo d'Alviano promulgated a military code intended to establish the spirit of the legions among the soldiers of St Mark. Officers and men were to swear allegiance to the Republic and forswear blasphemy, brawling and whoremongering; among other specific items, particularly fast horses were forbidden as a temptation to fly in the face of danger. Alviano was serious, too: in the summer of 1514 he had the noses slit of those prostitutes still found in camp. Reformers wanted more than new battle schemes; they were after a whole new military ethic.

The most famous and most influential Renaissance military theorist, Alviano's contemporary, Niccolò Machiavelli, took the emulation of Roman warfare to its farthest conclusion: he directly linked tactics to politics, musing that an infantry-based army, drilled and disciplined *all'antica*, could be the foundation of a virtuous neo-Roman republican state. Machiavelli published his military reform agenda – minus much of the republican politics – as *The Art of War* in 1521. It was his only major work to be published in his lifetime. It drew on three sources: Machiavelli's deep reading in the classics (Livy, Josephus, Tacitus, perhaps Polybius); his practical experience as the reorganizer of the Florentine republican militia; and his observation of the best military practice in the ongoing wars of Italy, including conversations with leading professional captains (Machiavelli briefly worked for Cesare Borgia). Though today Machiavelli's formulae for reform seem hopelessly ideal, based as they were on ancient Roman models, this was not the judgement of contemporaries: *The Art of War* was republished and translated several times during the sixteenth century – its idealism was not peculiar to its author, but an expression of a general Renaissance confidence in the possibility of a perfect synthesis of ancient and modern. It was this confidence, theoretical in Machiavelli, that guided the real-world projects of Bartolomeo d'Alviano, King Francis I, the Nassau cousins and others.

What made these marvellous sixteenth-century reform projects possible was a fascinating, coincidental similarity between the actual infantry practice of the late fifteenth century and the tactics of Greek and Roman infantry as described in surviving ancient texts. In fact because of this striking similarity, comparing ancient and modern infantry became practically unavoidable for anyone with any exposure to the military literature of Greece and Rome – and attempting the synthesis of past and present was merely the logical next step. This point needs careful explanation. The armies of the ancient world, according to the reformers' beloved texts, were dominated by disciplined regulation infantry units (maniples, cohorts, phalanxes) expertly ordered into any number of general-purpose and specialized formations: squares and rectangles, concave and convex crescents, wedges, rhomboids, even 'the scissors' and 'the tortoise' (in which Roman soldiers held interlocked shields over their heads to completely protect a unit from missiles). It was this precision and order, on the field and off, which appealed to Renaissance reformers – but wasn't this ancient discipline obviously inappropriate for warfare in the gunpowder age? In the minds of the reformers, no.

The arms of the ancient world were, of course, the sword and javelin of the Roman legionary, but in the case of the Macedonians of Alexander the Great (and in other Hellenistic Greek armies) the signature infantry weapon was the *sarissa*, a spear at least 15 feet long. Coincidentally enough, by the last quarter of the fifteenth century the most celebrated battlefield infantry in the Renaissance world, the Swiss, also used an extremely long spear, the pike. Here was a living connection between past and present, ancient and modern. Arranged in deep and broad squares amazingly similar to the ancient Greek phalanx formation, with the overlapping spears of several ranks all projecting forward, a Swiss pike unit presented an enemy with an awesome hedge of steel. Instilled with a ruthless warrior's code that ensured absolute battlefield discipline (instant death to any man who panicked), these Swiss pike squares won several notable victories in the late fifteenth century, particularly over the rich and powerful Duke Charles 'the Bold' of Burgundy at the battles of Grandson and Morat in 1476, and over the emperor Maximilian at the battle of Dornach in 1499.

These Swiss victories were by no means the first times since antiquity that infantry with long spears had won a battle (the Scots and Flemings as well as the Swiss had used pikes against their enemies in victories dating back to the early fourteenth century), but two circumstances made sure that the Swiss infantry tactics of the late fifteenth century became the basis of a new style of infantry warfare throughout Europe. First of all, from the end of the fifteenth century there were humanistic observers and reformers who instantly mentally connected a Swiss pike square with its ancient equivalents, the Greek phalanx or similar Roman formations. Secondly, the Swiss busily exported what became, particularly after their victories at Grandson and Morat, a trademark way of war. Poor men from a poor land, Swiss mercenaries by the thousand made a livelihood out of the pay and booty of foreign service: the cantons themselves managed a very profitable wholesale trade, while individual entrepreneurs organized a grey-market business in company-sized lots.

Duke Charles 'the Bold' of Burgundy besieges a Swiss force in Grandson, 1476. At the ensuing battle of Grandson the Swiss confederacy decisively defeated the crack forces of Duke Charles, and later in the same year they repeated the feat at Morat. These two victories first alerted Europe to the battlefield power of disciplined and ordered infantry.

The scarcity and expense of these Swiss mercenaries, as well as their reputation for arrogance, encouraged their duplication and replacement. In Germany, mercenary infantry companies known as *Landsknechts* (the word is uncertain in origin and meaning) learned to fight in the style of the Swiss, in broad and deep square formations using pikes, halberds (pole arms combining a spear point with axe blade) and immensely long two-handed swords wielded by 'double wage' men who embraced the glory and risks (as well as extra pay) of fighting in the front ranks. These landsknechts had their own cultural quirks, including strikingly aggressive, brightly-coloured costumes with exaggerated codpieces, oversized plumes, and puffy jackets and breeches slashed to reveal the cloth beneath. (This fashion for 'slashed' clothing was supposed to have originated when soldiers cut undersized, pillaged, luxury garments to make them fit – slashed outfits would go on to become a major civilian fashion trend of the century.) The first landsknecht companies were encouraged and hired, if not outright created, by the emperor Maximilian, who took them with him in his intervention in Italy in 1495. (And there a Venetian observer, writing in Latin, described a square of German pike as a 'phalanx' – the connection between ancient and modern was beginning to be made.) In Italy the German pikemen met and fought against the Swiss, whom they had already met in battle before: there was bad blood between the two groups, who are not always easily distinguishable in the sources. Evidence hints that at least some landsknechts were younger Swiss who had left their familial and cantonal loyalties behind: the feud between the two may well have been in part political and generational. In Italy, both 'Germans' and 'Swiss' also fought with and against French, Italian and Spanish infantry. Swiss and landsknecht also travelled farther afield, shifting wherever the winds of war blew them: a handful participated in the Castilian conquest of Granada, and some 2,000 German foot perished fighting for the Yorkist cause at the battle of Stoke in England in 1487, cut down by the massed archery of English longbowmen.

Though by no means a magic formula (as the defeat at Stoke shows), Swiss-style pike tactics travelled far, and were widely admired. Emulation naturally followed – most importantly in Italy. From 1495 Gonzalo de Cordoba, commander of the Spanish expeditionary force fighting in Naples, retrained his infantry after a sharp defeat at the hands of Swiss in French pay: a model for Gonzalo's reforms included 2,000 landsknechts lent him by the emperor Maximilian. Within a few years Spanish infantry would be considered as disciplined and tactically effective as any in Europe. At exactly the same time that Cordoba was reforming the Spanish infantry in southern Italy, in the Romagna the three Vitelli brothers, forward-thinking mercenary captains, trained a locally raised band to fight in the Swiss or German style, equipping them with extra-long pikes for good measure. In January 1497 Vitellozzo di Vitelli led a thousand of these men to victory against 800 German landsknechts in papal service.

But effectively copying Swiss or landsknecht organization and tactics was certainly not as easy as wishing for it. Issuing pikes was one thing, but teaching farm lads and apprentices how to confidently manage a long, ungainly weapon, and, most difficult of all, teaching them how to stand, march and move in synchrony, and believe in their collective strength even as the bullets whistled – all this was a very difficult enterprise. And how to do so without a cadre of Swiss or German professionals to do your training? And what if you didn't want to reproduce some of the more outlandish and difficult aspects of Swiss and landsknecht mercenary culture, along with their effective organization and tactics? Rulers and generals wanted the battlefield discipline and effectiveness of the new-style pike warfare – but not the camp-life problems of the Swiss and German mercenaries, with their penchant for negotiation and renegotiation, sudden strikes and other disobedience.

Here is where the ancient texts came to the fore. The observable similarities between ancient armies and modern-day Swiss – the pikes, the regular formations, the battlefield success – both suggested and encouraged a grand project to recover the whole of a lost and presumably superior ancient art of infantry war. Machiavelli was particularly fascinated by the parallel: in his *Art of War* he surmised that ancient military discipline had somehow survived intact in the isolated valleys of Switzerland, and in a 1513 letter he reported that the Swiss themselves compared their military skill with that of ancient Rome, and boasted that they could, if and when they wished, become the new masters of Italy. Indeed even as Machiavelli wrote, the Swiss were occupying Milan during a brief imperial moment (1512–15). The possibility of equating the Swiss way of war with the ancient lifted the problem of infantry tactics to the level of intellectual discussion, and made it worthy of written explication. This was an important development, for though the Swiss and the landsknechts certainly possessed elaborate, sophisticated and effective tactics, they apparently had almost nothing in the way of written, formal drill. Theirs was a culture of war, not a science – it was taught by old soldier to new, and was never really codified or regularized. (In fact, we have no evidence for any medieval written drill, including for Swiss pikemen or English archers.) But the moment infantry tactics became a problem for educated military men, as happened in Italy from the early sixteenth century, they naturally went about the problem in the manner of intellectuals: they talked, they corresponded, they wrote and they published. Their precious ancient texts, the scraps of a lost military science, naturally implied that the infantry manual was a legitimate literary genre – so they enthusiastically went about its renascence. They became modern Aelians. The resulting published treatises, some more touched by ancient knowledge than others, gave plenty of how-to detail, and further spread and encouraged a system of infantry war – an increasingly standardized system – all based on squares of pike.

So two reinforcing trends combined in Italy from the first decades of the sixteenth century: on the one hand there was a well-established tradition of practical mimesis, such as the landsknecht duplication of Swiss tactics, and Gonzalo de Cordoba's infantry reforms in Naples; and on the other hand the question of an ideal infantry captured the imagination of the more intellectual members of the military and policy élite – men like Alviano and Machiavelli who found it entirely appropriate to read a Roman author such as Josephus or Vegetius in the morning, and then apply a distillation of that reading to a real-world drill field in the afternoon. From this combination of experience and experiment emerged a consensus regarding the form and function of infantry. Renaissance military professionals came to agree that foot soldiers should march in step, they should be ordered in regular, gridded formations of ranks and files and they should be constantly, almost naggingly managed (in garrison, on the march, in battle) by a regular hierarchy of officers, including a new military social class of technical experts – sergeants.

When exactly in the course of the sixteenth century this standard infantry practice really coalesced is difficult to say. Past historians have tended to emphasize the national stories, carefully distinguishing between Swiss and German, Spanish and French. Differences certainly existed. But an assemblage of the remaining evidence hints that between the 1490s and the 1520s a remarkable cross-national and cross-ethnic pollination took place. Certainly by the mid century a Europe-wide infantry culture had been created, and so a Neapolitan sergeant serving the King of Spain in the Netherlands would be using, in general, the same techniques and vocabulary as a Gascon corporal drilling Frenchmen for the King of France. Importantly the underlying values at the heart of this standard practice – order, pattern, form, precision, repetition – were very similar to the principles disseminated, at the same time and among the same community, by the rules and regulations of angle bastion fortification. And like the spirit of the angle bastion, the spirit of the regular battalion would long outlast the particular circumstances of its invention in the Renaissance.

At the core of the new, standard infantry practice was the idea of a regular square of pike as the armature of every unit formation, and the foundation of a larger battlefield order in which an entire army was formed in multiple pike squares. In the phrase of the day the pike was the 'queen of battle', and it retained that distinction even as personal gunpowder weapons, the arquebus and then the heavier musket, became increasingly important on the battlefield. Though the pike appears a simple weapon, it is not a particularly natural one. Long and heavy, it took muscular strength and diligent practice to master. On the march the pike was more or less easily handled from its mid length balancing point; but in combat the soldier had to be able to project as much of the long shaft forward as possible while still holding the spear point steady. A wavering spear could not be well aimed, of course, and a formation of waving, clinking pikes would have advertised its wielders' collective unease, exhaustion or inexperience. Useful pike tactics took serious training. Recruits learned their basic weapons drill in groups of a half-dozen or so, under the eye of a corporal, an experienced soldier. Once they could handle a pike without knocking their neighbours down, small formation drill followed, say of a square of sixteen men in four rows and four ranks. And then came company and battalion drill, in units of a few hundred to a thousand men. Single mass formations could exceed five thousand men.

Units of this size, so impressive on parade and on the battlefield, were not easy to direct – or even to move at all. Men moving in ordered formations of several hundred or more cannot simply copy the motions of the man to left or right, front or back. Any large unit attempting to move on such a basis could only shamble forward, the ranks and files rippling and breaking as the men individually attempted to match their neighbours' motions. For a large regular formation to move steadily, and under the full control of its officers, every man must march in step, pacing, turning, starting and stopping at almost exactly the same moment. Such synchrony requires a cadence, a steady beat, and to provide this cadence massed drums proved ideal. Though military drumming seems an ancient thing, drums to regulate marching were a late-medieval innovation without precedence. Ancient armies had marched in step, but in time to singing – the Greek paean or war chant is an example – and the music of flutes and trumpets. Before the Swiss, there is only fleeting evidence of medieval soldiers marching in step at all. Significantly the sixteenth-century French military reformer Fourquevaux, who wrote to help refine King Francis I's legions experiment, specifically identified the Swiss as the inventors of the drum – the cadence of the drumbeat was yet another novel feature of the Swiss way of war, and an integral feature of the new infantry tactics. Drumming also added excitement, to be sure (Shakespeare's 'spirit-stirring drums'), but the new noise makers were introduced as practical tools of command, not for their musical or psychological qualities, however uplifting.

Training and cadence alone were not enough to maintain order. Enter the sergeant, who, in various ranks from corporal to sergeant major, managed the parts and the whole of a formally, properly arrayed army. On parade and on the battlefield the sergeants acted something like sheepdogs, constantly monitoring and adjusting the soldiers under their charge. The sergeant's job is made clear by the very vocabulary of the new infantry practice. The English word file, as in rank and file, comes from the Italian *file*, meaning 'threads' (originally there was no distinction between horizontal and vertical rows of men: both were termed files). A late sixteenth-century

A drummer, from a German print of 1599. No mere musician, the drummer played a critical role in the command and control of an ordered infantry formation. One infantry reformer compared the foot soldiers' necessary drumbeat to the whistling pipe used aboard galleys to ensure an even stroke – in both circumstances the only alternative to synchrony was chaos. The drum, no less than the pike or arquebus and musket, was a defining modernity of Renaissance infantry war.

manuscript translates the term *file* into 'strings' for 'Scottish' soldiers. A formation was thought of as a piece of cloth, a woven fabric, each thread being a line of men. The German term for sergeant makes the analogy clear: *Feldwebel* means 'field-weaver'. Period prints and paintings clearly show the sergeants at their work, weaving lines of men into disciplined squares, and holding them in those formations. In these illustrations the sergeants hover at the flanks, corners, front and rear of a unit, gesturing with an outstretched arm, sighting down the lines of men, holding their halberds horizontal at waist height to push the men straight. Doubtless they shouted vigorously, too. The sergeant's distinctive weapon, the halberd, was also a symbol and a tool, used something like a shepherd's crook. It could be used to guide the slow and the clumsy – or beat them. Though manuals advised patience it is clear that the full meaning of drill-field precision, to say nothing of basic discipline, was often taught with blows. Renaissance soldiering was, after all, a hard profession in a hard age.

From the perspective of the simple soldier the Renaissance sergeant was already what he remains to this day: an all-seeing eye, an enforcing hand. Yet the sergeant was no mere disciplinarian. His position demanded mental skills as well – surprisingly acute mental skills. Drill books agreed that sergeants should be both literate and numerate, really extraordinary qualifications at the time. Reading was necessary to help monitor army accounts and make sense

In late medieval warfare the halberd was a common infantry pole arm without particular significance. In the Renaissance it became the symbol and the tool of the sergeant, a low-level but important military professional with direct responsibility for ordering men in formation and ensuring discipline. Halberds also became associated with guards.

of written orders. Writing could help with the same. The mathematical demands on the sergeant were even more important. Consider a typical – actually a very simple – sixteenth-century tactical problem: a battalion of 1,600 pikemen, only 160 of them completely armoured with breastplates and helmets, to be put into a square with the best-equipped men in the front ranks. Since well-articulated, permanent sub-units had not yet been invented, the directing sergeants must give the orders that turn a milling crowd of 1,600 men into a perfect square of forty ranks and forty files. Calculating quickly, the sergeants separate the armoured from the unarmoured men and then have the corporals marshal the men into columns four files broad and forty ranks deep, with the first four ranks reserved for armoured men (forming a narrow column, one man after another, is relatively natural and easy). Thus the sergeants and their helpers produce ten manageable columns of 160 men each. Then the weaving commences. The first column is marched forward and halted. Then a second column is marched to the flank of the first column, and halted once its first rank reaches the first rank of the first column. The remaining eight columns follow in turn, each taking their place to the flank of the column that marched immediately before it. With all the columns lined up the corporals and sergeants busily set about the task of sighting down the ranks and files, setting them straight and making sure each and every man stands the same distance from his neighbours. The end result is a perfect square of 1,600 men, forty ranks by forty files, with the first four ranks being the best-armoured men.

In actual practice the art of weaving men into squares was considerably more complicated. Battalions in the field seldom numbered a perfect mathematical square (of 144, 169, 196 men and so on). Determining and then marshalling the leftover men – say, from a unit of 613 men arrayed with a frontage of thirteen files – took some computational skill. Sergeants had to keep track of not only the armoured and unarmoured pikemen but also the flag-bearers and drummers, who had to be placed in the marching columns so that they would end up at the centre of a marshalled square. And depending on the tactical situation, the desired 'square' formation might not be an exact square with the same number of ranks and files: among variations, there were 'double squares' with twice as many files as ranks, and then 'squares of ground' in which the square measured a perfect quadrilateral (for example, 50 feet by 50) but in which the ratio of ranks to files needed to be 3:7, because a marching man needs three paces of free room to his front and back, but only one pace to left and right. By this formula a formation of twenty-one men in three ranks and seven files (or of eighty-four men in six ranks and fourteen files) would have four sides of equal length. Fascinatingly the ratio of 3:7 repeatedly advocated in Renaissance manuals was exactly that recommended by the Roman tactician Vegetius – a clear example of a direct and sustained practical borrowing from the ancients.

To help prepare sergeants and other officers for the mathematical challenge of getting their formations right, drill books included methods for computing square roots. These hints could be quite sophisticated. One author, basing his system on the principle of the gnomon as discussed in Euclid's *Elements*, assured his readers that this method 'is very easy and manageable by the capacity of anyone'. He certainly assumed a very high level of mathematical knowledge among serving military men: was this faith exaggerated, or did sixteenth-century sergeants really have numeracy skills equal or superior to bookkeepers and bankers? Another writer adopted a technique from Tartaglia, one of the sixteenth century's greatest mathematicians. For those who had trouble with such calculations, in 1563 the Italian expert Girolomo Cataneo published a little guide to 'formations' – it was certainly one of the best-selling infantry manuals of the last third of the century – with page after page of elaborate tables listing all the various numbers relevant in forming squares, in different styles, out of units from 100 to many thousand men. The Spanish captain Valdes thought this book 'very useful especially to those who don't have much skill at figures'. There were other aids. Sergeant majors carried a baton for pointing, and a few

Veteran landsknecht sergeants and officer: a woodcut from a German treatise of 1555. In the mid sixteenth century the battlefield reputation of the German mercenary landsknecht bands was second to none. They were even more famous for their exaggerated costumes, a kind of visual braggadocio. These figures sport the typical landsknecht finery, with slashed sleeves and pantaloons cut to ribbons. In life these garments would have been brightly coloured.

surviving examples have tables of square roots engraved along their barrels. The great astronomer Galileo, who taught classes in military mathematics, went to the effort of designing a military compass or protractor, an actual instrument to be fabricated in brass and used on the battlefield as a sort of slide rule for quickly and accurately performing advanced calculations. By the end of the sixteenth century soldiering, even at the most basic level of infantry tactics, had become a real science, imagined and managed with numbers.

Over the same decades that the Swiss and landsknechts established the reputation of the pike it became equally clear that gunpowder weapons had become an important part of infantry warfare. This is not to say that traditional bowed weapons became obsolete. A crossbow could probably shoot with almost as much deadly force as a gun and could be aimed with greater accuracy. Though the crossbow's maximum range may well have been less than that of a gun, their effective ranges essentially overlapped. There is evidence that soldiers preferred a firearm to a bow. Was there a sense of fun, or other psychological satisfaction, connected with blasting away? Interestingly one advantage of the gun was in terms of endurance: a soldier could easily carry more powder and bullets than crossbow bolts, meaning that a firearm could be discharged more often than a bow. But most importantly guns were simply cheaper than crossbows. A gun barrel was only a tube of iron, while the bow of a crossbow had to be made from high-quality spring steel, and the necessary crank or lever apparatus needed to bend a steel bow was probably more expensive to make than the simple lock of an early firearm. And so, for reasons of cost and perhaps fashion as much as performance, firearms gradually replaced the traditional bowed missile weapons of Europe. But not everywhere, and not overnight.

In Great Britain the longbow remained common into the last decades of the sixteenth century, when there was a vigorous print debate between defenders of the ancestral bow and advocates of its suppression. Firearms enthusiasts argued that a musket shot was more murderous, but the real problem with the longbow was that it took bodily strength and years of practice to master. The more

Opposite: *In a detail from an early sixteenth-century painting by Hans Holbein the elder, a soldier uses a claw and crank mechanism to pull back the steel bow of his crossbow. He will load his weapon with the bolt or quarrel he holds in his teeth. Military crossbows were both accurate and powerful, but slow to load, and their steel bows and complex crank mechanisms were expensive and difficult to manufacture. Firearms were simpler and cheaper.*

mechanically complex gun paradoxically took less skill. A testament to this fact comes from a mid sixteenth-century English merchant adventurer to the Guinea Coast of Africa, who found that the local men were not strong enough to pull back a longbow's bowstring – but the same Englishman's landing party was chased off by local inhabitants using firearms supplied by earlier Portuguese traders. The longbow survived in corners of the British Isles into the seventeenth century. Among its very last martial users were in a party of Scots acquired to assist at the defence of Stralsund in the Baltic in 1628. On the continent the crossbow practically disappeared as a weapon by 1550.

The standard infantry firearm from the very late fifteenth century was the arquebus, a thickly stocked weapon with a barrel about a metre long. The earliest personal firearms had been fired from the chest, or tucked under the arm, discharged by the user touching a red-hot pricker to a small hole at the rear of the barrel. The more sophisticated arquebus was fired by a matchlock mechanism, in which a smouldering length of match (a slow-burning cord saturated with saltpetre) was held in the jaws of a lever bolted to the stock of the gun. When the soldier pulled the gun's trigger a spring snapped this lever back, bringing the burning match against a sprinkling of powder held in a small pan or dimple. The flash of powder in this pan penetrated a small hole in the barrel to ignite the charge and fire the gun. From the mid sixteenth century on a heavier infantry firearm, the musket, became more common. It was so long and awkward that it had to be fired from a forked rest the soldier stuck in the ground before him. (The term 'musket' could also refer to very heavy infantry guns, common in sieges, fired from tripods or other supports.) The standard infantry musket was a truly powerful weapon. In 1591 Humphrey Barwick stated that a lead musket ball could penetrate the best armour at 200 yards, ordinary armour at 400, and kill an unarmoured man at 600. Of course the trick was to hit what was aimed at. The average musket or arquebus was extremely inaccurate, meaning that the

A scene inside an armoury of Emperor Maximilian I, a manuscript painting by Jörg Kolderer, c. 1512. A soldier uses a red-hot pricker to fire a large musket mounted on a stout wooden tripod. Smaller muskets carried by a single infantryman first appeared in North Italy in the 1520s. Heavier, more powerful, and with a greater range than a standard arquebus, these infantry muskets were fired from a forked rest.

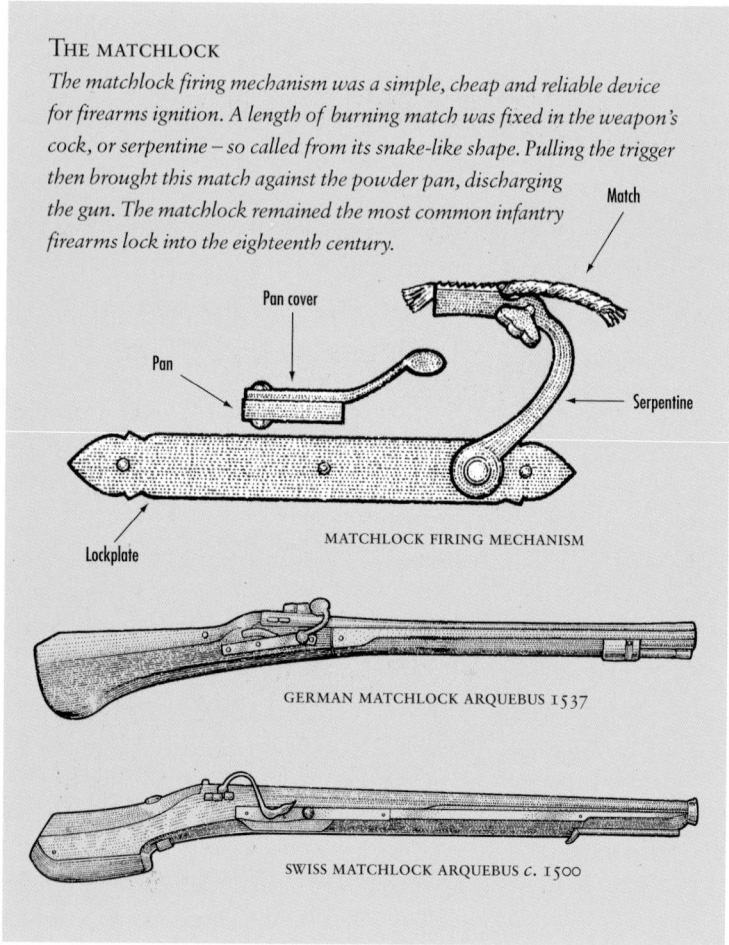

THE MATCHLOCK

The matchlock firing mechanism was a simple, cheap and reliable device for firearms ignition. A length of burning match was fixed in the weapon's cock, or serpentine – so called from its snake-like shape. Pulling the trigger then brought this match against the powder pan, discharging the gun. The matchlock remained the most common infantry firearms lock into the eighteenth century.

Match

Pan cover

Pan

Serpentine

Lockplate

MATCHLOCK FIRING MECHANISM

GERMAN MATCHLOCK ARQUEBUS 1537

SWISS MATCHLOCK ARQUEBUS *c.* 1500

effective range for aimed fire was closer to 100–200 yards than to any theoretical maximum – which is not to say that many an unlucky man was not killed by a randomly fired bullet at much greater distances. Rifled guns did already exist, with grooves cut into the interior of the barrel to spin a bullet in flight and so guide it more truly. They were specialized sniper's weapons.

The introduction of firearms was only coincident with the development of disciplined tactics based on ordered formations. There was nothing particular to the arquebus or the musket, as compared with a crossbow or longbow, to encourage the new tactics. Indeed reconciling firearms to the new tactics took considerable ingenuity. Why bother? Though a cloud of skirmishers might be no less likely to shoot at the enemy, and shoot well, than a solid body of men, they have one grave defect from the point of view of a general or a sergeant – once deployed they can hardly be managed or controlled as the battle unfolds. So even as the ratio of men armed with firearms matched and then surpassed those armed with pike, tacticians clung to their pike squares and the proven techniques of rank and file drill. Also, without the protection of nearby pikes, infantry armed with the slow-loading arquebus or musket were vulnerable prey to any swift-riding cavalry that should chance to swoop down on them. On the other hand a square of disciplined pike was practically invulnerable to cavalry attack. The natural solution was to keep shot close to pike. According to one expert up to five ranks of arquebusiers or musketeers could be sheltered within the reach of lowered pikes.

Attaching troops armed with firearms to squares of pike introduced a new level of tactical complexity to the art of infantry management. One relatively easy technique was to include a few ranks of shot near the front of a pike square. But shot locked towards the interior of a square could only fire when the enemy was almost within pike-touch. There were two more sophisticated alternatives, both of which allowed considerable offensive fire: sleeves and horns. A sleeve was simply a few files of shot placed on one or both flanks of the pike square. Horns took a great deal more skill. A horn was a separate, small square of arquebusiers or musketeers placed at the corner of a larger pike square. Typically a pike square would have four horns, one at each corner, but sometimes there were only two, one to the right and one to the left front. Maintaining perfect form as a large pike square with four large horns walked across the undulating ground of a battlefield must have stretched the professional skills of both soldiers and hectoring sergeants to the limit. Such a formation, with all its implications of military perfection, might also have sent a shiver of concern through a body of less experienced or less well-drilled adversaries.

Though strange indeed to eyes more accustomed to the long lines of seventeenth-century and later infantry tactics, the squares and horns of Renaissance infantry war had their own logic. On the battlefield the presiding sergeant major, working with his commanding general, marshalled his separate battalions, each a square of pike with sleeves or horns of shot, in chequerboard fashion with wide open gaps between the units. There was considerable scope for imagination and experiment in these army arrays. The Italian Giovacchino da Coniano, sergeant major under King Henry VIII of England in the 1540s, had thirty-two different schemes. The open spaces between the units were functionally very important; these were fire lanes for the arquebusiers and musketeers to shoot along. If cleverly arrayed and properly spaced the fire from one battalion could flank and support its neighbours. This enthusiasm for flanking fire was of course borrowed from military architecture. Sixteenth-century tacticians even imagined a square with horns formation being the walking, human equivalent of a citadel with bastions. Robert Barrett explained this to his (presumably backward) English compatriots in his 1598 *Theory and Practice of Modern War*: 'a well framed battle or squadron of pikes, well impaled with shot, and angled with squadrons of Muskets, seems a Castle ... [and if] framed of expert and resolute men, is of wonderful force'. Now in truth a square of human beings could hardly be flanked by fire in the same way as inanimate walls and bastions, but contemporaries still clung to the possibility that schemes for maximizing flanking fire would lead to the perfection of infantry tactics. There was another solution to the problem of adapting firearms to the rank and file grid of pike-square tactics: the countermarch, which allowed many ranks of shot to fire effectively without any need for wide fire lanes between units. In the countermarch the first man in a file fired and then wheeled to walk

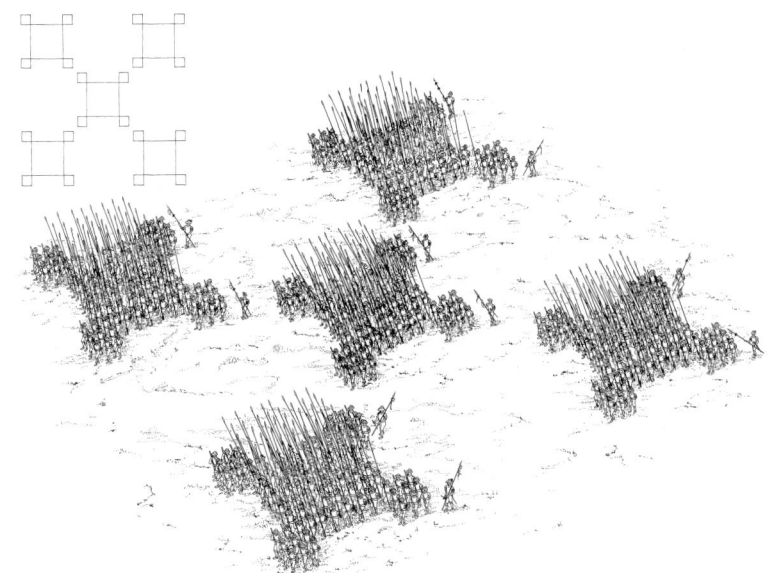

INFANTRY SQUARES WITH HORNS
A line drawing diagram of five battalions, each a square of pikemen with four horns of shot (either arquebusiers or musketeers). Army formations of this complexity were not just parade-day exercises but actual battlefield tactics. From the point of view of a Renaissance general or sergeant major each square with horns was a walking castle, with the four horns providing flanking fire to all sides. A chequered formation of battalions ensured zones of overlapping fire between the battalions. The drawing is not to scale. Actual distances between battalions would have been around 50 metres.

back to the end of his file (moving through the space between files). Meanwhile the next man in line stepped forward and fired. The men in the rearward files, waiting their turn to fire, would busy themselves with the many steps of loading their weapons. By this system a unit could stand still, or even slowly advance or retreat, all the time shooting forth a steady volume of fire. The invention of the countermarch is usually credited to the Nassau cousins at the end of the sixteenth century, but the underlying motions of the drill, with files rotating front to back, was identical with an evolution called the limaçon or caracole that can be traced back to at least the 1490s. In the seventeenth century the countermarch (along with increasing concentration on maximizing the speed of reloading) would help encourage the creation of more linear tactics with thinner formations and smaller and smaller gaps between units until, in the eighteenth century, an entire army could muster for battle standing almost shoulder to shoulder and only three or four ranks deep. In the sixteenth century, though the effort is usually discredited, it was mounted troops that first adopted ordered tactics for providing a continuous forward fire: the cavalry caracole.

THE WAR WAGON

There was an alternative to the new infantry tactics of pike and shot: the war wagon. Infantry using heavy wagons for cover were as invulnerable to cavalry attack as a well-disciplined pike square, and crossbowmen or arquebusiers could shoot from the protection of loopholes cut in the heavy board siding. Some wagons mounted small cannon, to fire either forward or sideways from behind sliding wooden screens. A laager of these wagons, alternating with artillery pieces, made a fine camp defence or battlefield strongpoint.

The perfecters, if not the inventors, of wagon tactics were the Czech Hussites in the 1420s and the Hungarians of a generation later. Though generally overlooked, the use of war wagons persisted throughout the sixteenth century, and in Western Europe. At the battle of Ravenna (1512) the Spanish had at least thirty carts mounting scythe blades, forward-projecting spears and organ guns. Henry VIII of England had twenty wagons, again fitted with scythe blades, in his camp at Boulogne (1544). The defenders at Haarlem (1573) sallied under the cover of a line of wheeled 'wooden sconces' spread between five and ten paces apart. The Portuguese army used wagons at Alcazarquivir (1578) in Morocco. Leonardo da Vinci's famous circular wooden tank with multiple gun ports was the war wagon at its most refined.

Fascinatingly, unlike the tactics of rank and file, the tactics of the war wagon spread far beyond Christian Europe. The Ottomans – who never

*A late fifteenth-century Imperial camp defended by a laager of war wagons,
each with a small artillery piece protected by sliding wooden doors. These
wagons are more like screens than mobile block houses.*

adopted the pike – encountered wagon defences in their fifteenth-century
wars against Hungary, where they learned to bind artillery together with
mantlets and wagons to protect infantry. Turkish mercenaries brought
these techniques farther east, notably at the battle of Panipat in India
(1526), where the Moguls crushed the Delhi sultanate. Given the pace of
this eastward progress, it is just possible that Hussite wagons were the
original idea behind the military reformer Ch'i Chi'kuang's widespread
introduction of war wagons to the Imperial Chinese army in 1568.

In Europe war wagons were used at least until the battles of Wimpfen
(1622) and Wittstock (1636) during the Thirty Years War.

CHAPTER THREE

The New Caesars

Infantry and artillery were the hammer and anvil of modern Renaissance warfare, but there was still a battlefield place for the man-at-arms, the aristocratic heavy cavalryman. Mounted on a powerful charger, wearing a full suit of armour, and trained from boyhood to wield a lance with deadly skill, the man-at-arms was an expert combatant, and in company with his peers he remained a powerful battlefield presence. But even as the military skills of the knight reached their apotheosis, the culture of Europe's nobility was changing. The ancient example, that of Greece and Rome, was now ascendant. Under that influence, Europe's military élite increasingly styled themselves as modern-day Caesars – as generals rather than warriors.

The New Caesars

THE RENAISSANCE TRANSFORMATION of warfare challenged Europe's traditional military élite – the knightly aristocracy – to reconsider and reinvent their place and purpose on the battlefield. This challenge was a subtle one. It was not the coming of gunpowder, nor the new military architecture, nor the new infantry tactics that directly threatened the existence or importance of the old, medieval military élite (who were, of course, Europe's social and political élite as well). Indeed, with exceptions, the nobility would continue to dominate the leadership of European states and armies for centuries to come, at least until the French and industrial revolutions, and in many circumstances well into the twentieth century. During the Renaissance military, technical and tactical changes caused no real social or political revolution in the control of war. In fact the Renaissance transformation of warfare was only made possible by the enthusiasm of the old élite for new weapons and new techniques, and this passion for experiment in no way entailed a conscious rejection of any medieval military heritage. Innovation and tradition comfortably coexisted. An example of this ease comes in the person of King Henry VIII of England, who both collected firearms and practised his archery, and who hired Italian captains to modernize his soldiers' infantry drill while importing German craftsmen to manufacture exquisite custom-made suits of armour. It is also worth remembering that almost every single major military reformer of the period was a titled noble by birth.

However, even as Renaissance Europe's military aristocracy continued to monopolize the direction of warfare (and continued to honour the martial traditions of their ancestors), the terms of that power gradually but dramatically changed. By the end of the sixteenth century the nobility exercised their long-standing control over warfare in very different ways than had their great-grandfathers of the previous century. At least in theory, the battlefield of the fifteenth century was socially stratified, with noble and commoner differently armed and organizationally separated. Ideally a noble fought on horseback, properly armoured and properly armed with lance and sword. He disdained missile weapons, openly lusted after the thrill of combat, and expected to fight within a company of his peers. On the battlefield he preferred to confront opponents of equal rank. In contrast, a commoner fought on foot with bow or pole arm. He, too, fought beside his peers, but peers of a humbler sort than the noble man-at-arms – say, fellow members of a town or district militia. His role on the battlefield, in the eyes of his social superiors, was decidedly subordinate to the knights and barons on their plunging chargers.

There were, it is important to note, many practical exceptions to this theoretical segregation. At Agincourt in 1415 most of the English men-at-arms dismounted and arrayed themselves with the archers and other foot, the better to withstand charges by mounted French knights. Seven years later, at Arbedo in North Italy, armoured Milanese men-at-arms, after several fruitless horsed charges, dismounted to attack and defeat a Swiss force of infantry (as yet only partially armed with pikes). Such sensible tactical expedients were indeed rather common, and there were many general situations – siege warfare being the most obvious – where the ideal separation of horsed knight from commoner footman was impossible. Yet a sense of warfare as existing on two levels, the one honourable and the other less so, persisted among the aristocracy, and the formal organization of armies continued to reflect this imagined moral difference, with the nobility clustering in separate companies of heavy horsemen.

Complete outfit of armour for a man-at-arms and his horse, manufactured by the Antwerp maker Eliseus Libaerts, c. 1560.

This medieval military segregation, by birth and by type, eroded over the course of the sixteenth century, changing in two ways. First of all, chivalry evolved into cavalry as the mounted arm became more a separate branch of service and less the military expression of the ruling class. Second, the military nobility more generally evolved into an officer corps, exercising their leadership as a hierarchy of office-holders stretching down from the commander-in-chief through all the units of an army, including the infantry. Importantly, the nature and activity of the commander-in-chief changed significantly as well: battlefield example mattered less, generalship more. The art of managing and directing an army – in camp, on the march, on the battlefield – became a commander's greatest responsibility, and his skill at these tasks the measure of his worth. Bravery still mattered and personal skill at arms remained respected, but, at least among the higher echelons of the officer aristocrats, warfare was now an intellectual problem, not an athletic exercise. War was no longer controlled from the back of a horse, lance in hand at the head of a squadron, but from table tops strewn with maps and city plans, muster receipts and detailed lists of stores. The model of the perfect military type shifted as well, away from the literary hero – Roland, David, Amadis of Gaul – and towards the ancient historical general: Alexander, Scipio, Julius Caesar.

It took several generations for the mounted man-at-arms to lose his battlefield pre-eminence. Through at least the first half of the sixteenth century the well-born, well-equipped aristocratic horseman was broadly assumed to be the single most powerful combatant on the battlefield, and companies of such men were the most prestigious units of an army. More than tradition ensured this respect: the Renaissance man-at-arms was a genuinely fearsome warrior, the product of over five hundred years of refinement in horse breeding, armour manufacture and weapons training. Not the least of his authority flowed from his magnificent fighting partner, the stamping and snorting warhorse, a carefully bred balance of speed, strength and stamina. Such mounts were expensive to purchase, but also to maintain. Large and difficult

The French army of King Louis XII skirmishes outside Genoa in 1507; from an illuminated manuscript, c. 1510. A fully caparisoned company of noble men-at-arms was a gorgeous sight, with stamping steeds, shining armour and yards and yards of rich fabric coverings. Such glory did not come cheap. The properly equipped warrior aristocrat needed a mountain of equipment, all of it expensive to purchase and equally expensive to maintain.

pure-breds, they ate a mountain of fodder, and each had its own groom, who often doubled as a man-servant (there was no question of a man-at-arms curry-combing his own horse or fetching his own dinner).

The man-at-arms' defensive equipment, his armour, was no relic of a previous age. Armour manufacture reached its pinnacle in the Renaissance, the two leading regions of production being southern Germany and North Italy. From the workshops of Milan and Brescia, Augsburg and Nuremberg, master armourers with Europe-wide reputations produced elaborate, fully articulated suits of overlapping steel plates, each suit a near-perfect marriage of form and function. So-called parade armours not necessarily intended for combat were often completely covered with beautifully engraved designs in the best modern taste, sometimes inlaid with gold. But even the plainer armours were

A sixteenth-century armourer's shop, from an engraving by Stradanus. Armour had its high end, its haute couture; it also had its shops of relative mass production. Here a bank of grinding wheels stands ready for workers to polish and take the edge off freshly forged armour. The gearing mechanism in the lower left of the print would have connected the grinding wheels with a waterwheel below or beside the shop. For the sixteenth century this was a considerable industrial establishment.

magnificent works of hammer and anvil, especially considering the design constraints on their makers. An armourer had to exactly match each piece of steel to the shape and vulnerability of the body part protected, and there was always an understanding that weight had to be balanced against strength. Apparent design flourishes often turn out to be deeply functional. For example, the fluted, folded shapes of German armours in the 'Maximilian' style (after Emperor Maximilian I) were not only decorative, but added stiffness and thus strength without increasing weight. Though not perfect, a good suit of armour would blunt or deflect all but the most well-aimed lance, or the most direct crossbow bolt or arquebus bullet. In the second half of the sixteenth century, as firearms became a more dreaded battlefield killer (especially as horsemen adopted the pistol), the most vital pieces of armour increased in thickness, and it became common to 'proof' a breastplate by firing a shot against it at point-blank range. The resulting dimple was not pounded out, but retained to assure the purchaser of the steel's strength. Arquebus-proof breastplates were naturally heavier than those warranted merely pistol-proof. Thanks to the ingenuity and skill of the Renaissance armourer, even at its protective peak combat armour never overly encumbered the wearer: a fully armoured man-at-arms could always mount his horse himself, and could easily twist and turn in the saddle, or raise his arm overhead. (Tournament armour was much more burdensome and restricting, with the helmet sometimes bolted to the cuirass for added safety against impact and whiplash, but of course such suits were never intended for use in war.) Battle armour was not reserved for man alone: barding covered the head, neck, chest and hindquarters of the man-at-arms' horse.

The man-at-arms' prime weapon remained the heavy lance. Much like the longbow, this was a mechanically simple weapon that was none the less very difficult to master. It took talent and years of training to develop the strength and balance to sit a charging horse while holding a lance firm and steady. The ideal aiming point was the head or neck of the mounted opponent. Jousts remained a popular event, a chance for well-born warriors to display their hard-won skill. At a 1559 tourney held to celebrate peace between France and Spain, King Henry II of France was tragically killed by a spectacularly well-aimed lance that splintered against his visor, sending a shard of wood through the vision-slit to pierce his eye and brain. This blow was delivered in a tournament, but equal skill was possible on the battlefield. At Fornovo in 1495, according to a Venetian observer who was also a curious medical doctor, many of the dead men-at-arms were mortally wounded by a precise lance blow to the neck. Such brutal precision, delivered by one man moving at speed against another, required practice from boyhood. The lance had its limitations. It could only be used at first contact with the enemy, and only at the culmination of a mounted charge. It was a one-time weapon. Unless the wielder completely missed his target, or his weapon glanced aside, a lance shattered on impact – a testament to the force involved. The Florentine painter Paolo Uccello littered the foreground of his paintings of the battle of San Romano with the discarded stumps and pieces of broken lances. In the moments after a charge, in the clutch of mêlée combat, the man-at-arms relied on his sword. Armour-cracking maces and war hammers were also popular.

Besides his specialized equipment and extensive training, the traditional man-at-arms brought his own peculiar view of warfare to the battlefield. Foremost in his mind was the possibility of acquiring renown through combat. This personal mission could sometimes overshadow any sense of the larger strategy in play or politics at stake. Baldassare Castiglione, who captained a squadron of fifty men-at-arms at the turn of the sixteenth century, recommended in his immensely influential book of manners, *The Courtier*, that a man should only put himself in danger when there was the possibility of his individual bravery being noticed and talked about. Such an admission suggests the extent to which the psychology of the tournament coloured real war: for the warrior aristocrat, there had to be spectators. War and tourney could indeed become substantially blurred. During a truce at the siege of Barletta in 1503 thirteen French and thirteen Spanish knights agreed to an arranged combat. At the first charge the Spanish men-at-arms aimed at the horses of their French opponents, killing eleven, and outraging the French knights – the smaller points of chivalric martial etiquette were obviously quite different on either side of the Pyrenees. Amazingly the French knights went on to win the encounter. One of the French heroes at Barletta, the Chevalier de Bayard, became the subject of a little memoir, the *Loyal Servitor*, that lovingly described his personal feats of arms while ignoring such issues as whether a battle was won or lost. To Bayard the difference was perhaps negligible. He died in the saddle in 1524 – as had most heads of his family for the past two hundred years – felled by an arquebus ball as he charged the enemy in the closing stages of a battle already lost (Bayard was in fact the commander of the defeated force). Such vainglory was increasingly understood to be foolish, even a kind of ill discipline. At the end of the sixteenth century Cervantes (who knew war well, having lost an arm at the battle of Lepanto in 1571), parodied the chivalric pretensions of an earlier generation in his novel *Don Quixote*. Tilting at windmills had no place on the disciplined modern battlefield.

Even when a paragon of restraint, the man-at-arms had other drawbacks and liabilities. Most importantly, on a per capita basis he was exceedingly expensive, both for the state and for the man-at-arms himself. As a man of rank and property (at least in theory), he was expected to provide his own horse, armour and other gear (which could be extensive), as well as that of his servants and assistants. Of course the aristocratic ethos ensured much costly competition in livery and other finery. In many cases a man-at-arms' pay only subsidized the heavy financial burdens of going to war as a gentleman. Besides the expense, a man-at-arms was not a versatile combatant. Outside of the rare battlefield clash his specialized equipment and skills were a near-useless premium. In fact the clattering companies of men-of-arms were perhaps most useful for triumphal entries and on other ceremonial occasions, when their plumes and pedigreed steeds materially added to the prestige of their masters and employers. For scouting, foraging, guarding bridges and crossroads, and the many other mundane duties of ordinary campaigning, lighter and less culturally burdened types of cavalry proved they could do the job both better and more cheaply.

By the beginning of the sixteenth century there were several different types of light horse, many of them originating in the frontier regions of Europe. In Spain the raiding warfare of the Reconquista produced the *jinetas*, or genitors, javelin-armed skirmishers. Interestingly this native light cavalry tradition seems to have died out within a generation of the fall of Granada in 1492, the end of the Iberian frontier between Christian and Muslim. In the poor far north of England there were the border horse, simply equipped with quilted jacket or mail shirt, steel hat and spear. Henry VIII found them invaluable on his continental adventures, his daughter Elizabeth I in the project of pacifying Ireland, another frontier zone. Venice extensively recruited light cavalry from her Balkan possessions in Greece and Albania. These were the infamous stradiots, armed with light lances and sabres, who excelled at the complementary techniques of raiding and looting. Their ethnic and religious origins were suspect, and some were undoubtedly born Muslims – the troop of Turkish light horse that defected during the Otranto campaign of 1481 were probably classed as stradiots. Croats, Pandours and Hungarian hussars were similar types of Eastern light cavalry. Venice was often their first Western employer, but troops soon passed into the service of other states. Throughout the period the most aggressive and effective light horse came from Europe's borderlands, where savage, scuffling encounters were of course a way of life. The martial techniques of all these different frontiersmen were astonishingly similar: in 1551 a Venetian described English border horse as being armed like Albanians. There were other, less exotic types of light cavalry in Renaissance armies. It is unclear whether mounted crossbowmen, and the mounted arquebusiers who replaced them, fought more from horseback or were really mounted infantry. Like their seventeenth-century descendants, the dragoons, their deployment probably depended on the immediate situation. They were invaluable for ambuscades, escorts and other small operations. None of these various types of light cavalry could face men-at-arms on the battlefield.

A new type of heavy horsemen first appeared in Germany in the 1540s, the *reiters* or ritters. These had abandoned the lance for the pistol, a short-barrelled firearm light enough to be wielded with one hand even from a moving horse. The critical technical innovation was not the pistol's length but its clockwork firing mechanism, the wheel lock. To ready his weapon the pistoleer used a wrench or spanner to

THE WHEEL LOCK

The matchlock firearm, with its long and smouldering length of match, was really a two-handed weapon and generally unsuitable for use on horseback. The invention of the wheel lock, and its use on a short-barrelled gun, the pistol, brought cavalry into the gunpowder age. Ignited by sparks flying from a lump of iron pyrites brought against a spinning serrated wheel, a wheel-lock firearm could be loaded and wound tight in advance and then fired at will. In the second half of the sixteeenth century the mounted pistoleer gradually replaced the lance-armed man-at-arms.

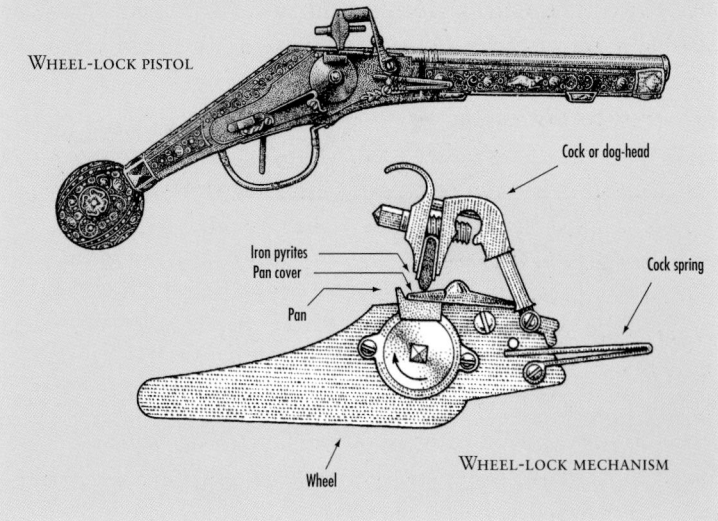

WHEEL-LOCK PISTOL

Cock or dog-head

Iron pyrites
Pan cover

Cock spring

Pan

Wheel

WHEEL-LOCK MECHANISM

crank a serrated wheel against a stiff spring until a small nut engaged the wheel and held it in check. Pulling the trigger then released this nut, spinning the serrated wheel against a lump of pyrites to produce a shower of sparks into the powder pan, thus firing the gun. Once loaded and wound, a wheel-lock pistol could be held until needed – and then steadied and fired with one hand. Because they were a more expensive and more finicky weapon than the rude matchlock, wheel locks tended to be limited to cavalry and sporting guns. Each reiter rode into battle with at least a brace of wheel-lock pistols in his saddle holsters; some boasted three or four or more, the extras tucked into belts and boot-tops. Some also had a longer-barrelled gun slung over the shoulder. Besides firearms, each horseman carried a long, stout stabbing sword, the estoc, and a dagger. In short, they were armed to the teeth. Reiters wore complete or nearly complete suits of armour – fashionably blackened. This touch gave them their nickname of 'black riders' or 'devil riders'. An unusually sharp appetite for plunder helped darken their reputation as well. Horses were unbarded.

The tactics of the reiters were as innovative as their weapons. Their speciality was the fire drill called the caracole, a term apparently borrowed from infantry practice. (The extent to which the infantry

A wheel-lock pistol from the second half of the sixteenth century. Like almost all firearms of the period the wheel-lock pistol was a muzzle-loading weapon. More expensive than the rude matchlock, the wheel lock was rarely used for infantry weapons, though a few high-end arquebuses and muskets were equipped with the fancier locks. Some of these had rifled barrels, and a very few were even breech-loading. On the battlefield these guns would have made excellent sniping weapons.

caracole was also a drill for fire management, rather than just a technique for movement, is unclear.) In the cavalry caracole, a deep but relatively narrow formation of reiters halted in front of their target, but well beyond the effective range of retaliatory small arms fire. Successive ranks of pistoleers then trotted to within point-blank pistol distance, discharged their guns, wheeled and returned to the back of the formation to reload and wait until their rank was once again the foremost. When performed with discipline the caracole must have produced a withering stream of constant fire, particularly against a formation of infantry standing in open ground. It is hard to imagine the caracole being used against fellow cavalry, but there was no question of the reiters flinching at a confrontation with lance-armed men-at-arms. Indeed in the second half of the sixteenth century the clash of pistoleer and lancer created a debate over the proper arming of heavy cavalry.

Some aristocratic contemporaries found the new weapons and new tactics of the German reiters disturbing. The pistol had unsavoury connections. Its handiness appealed to criminals as well as horsemen, and many states banned firearms of less than a certain length as a threat against law and order. One Italian damned the pistol as a weapon fit only for assassins, and certainly it was the weapon of choice in many of the political killings of the second half of the sixteenth century, including the murders of Francis of Guise, leader of the French Catholics, in 1563, and William of Orange, leader of the Dutch Protestants, in 1584. If some found the pistol distasteful, others admired the reiters' battlefield courage and acknowledged the effect of a close-range, mass pistol discharge. The French captain Blaise de Montluc described what it was like to meet them in battle: 'one could see nothing but fire and steel'. Montluc also noted the reiters' personal attention to their horses, their quick reaction to alarms, their ability to seize and defend villages; in short, their overall versatility. And unlike the lance-armed men-at-arms, on the battlefield the reiters could confront pike-armed infantry as well as fellow heavy cavalry. Historians have sometimes sympathized with late sixteenth-century arguments in favour of retaining the lance, but the blunt fact is that the pistol won out. The pistoleer spread from Germany to France and Italy and became the most numerous cavalry type. From the last third of the sixteenth century the remaining companies of men-at-arms increasingly abandoned their lance to take up pistols, and with this conversion the old social primacy of the man-at-arms was lost as well. In the next century a curmudgeonly Scot lamented that 'the ancient distinction between cavalry and infantry, as to their birth and breeding, is wholly taken away'.

Europe's old military aristocracy, decreasingly self-segregated within the companies of men-at-arms, meanwhile evolved into an officer class. A universally recognized hierarchy of command developed that was particularly important among the infantry, whose neatly ordered march columns and battlefield squares were now the ruling forms of battlefield warfare. These formations demanded two reinforcing kinds of leadership, both moral and technical, and on both the unit and army levels. A young man of birth and ambition began his career by joining a company – often commanded by a neighbour or a relative – and serving as a lieutenant or an ensign, the latter literally with responsibility to carry the unit flag. In Spain, where the nobility was both numerous and poor, it was not uncommon or disgraceful for a young man to enlist as a simple pikeman. He might then rise as high as courage, skill and patronage could lift him. A captain commanded a company, typically from one hundred to three hundred men. For combat, companies were grouped together to make battalions, as yet a technical tactical term and not a permanent organizational structure. (Organizationally companies might be ordered into regiments or, in Spanish or Italian armies, tercios.) In charge of a battalion was the colonel. In higher command there was the general, assisted by an informal staff, most importantly a council of war including the army's colonels and other respected and experienced officers. The sergeant major (at this time a senior officer in charge of sergeants, not a senior sergeant) assisted the general in communicating a plan of battle to the technical experts, the sergeants, responsible for actually marshalling the men in formation.

At the lower levels of army organization the lieutenants, company captain, and battalion colonels helped direct the sergeants in performing the work of maintaining order among the ranks and files. These officers also provided situational direction, that is tactical decision-making (such as detailing a detachment of shot to hold a ditch or seize a farmhouse), but their defining contribution was moral leadership. The old reckless bravery of the medieval knight was sublimated into a steelier, more passive – and perhaps even more demanding – battlefield ethic, a new kind of physical courage that was simultaneously a code of conduct and a language of command. According to this code the officer had to be both conspicuous and insensible to possible injury. An officer was always expected to stand at the head of his company or battalion, coolly daring the enemy marksmen to take their aim at his towering plume or flowing sash (King Henry IV of France, whose military instincts were firmly those of a junior officer, habitually wore a gigantic white feather, his famous panache). Though an officer, unlike most rankers, often enjoyed the protection of a good-quality helmet, a breastplate with attached tassets to protect the thigh, and sometimes a small shield, all our available evidence suggests that tactical officers died in extraordinary numbers: eleven of the twelve Spanish colonels at Ravenna (1512), for example. At the siege of Rouen in 1563 just under 50 per cent of the officers and sergeants of seventeen Catholic infantry companies were wounded enough for the fact to be noted (the percentage of the remaining 50 per cent who were killed outright is unknown). Sangfroid, rather than a hot temper, was the gentleman officer's crowning virtue. Brantôme, whose *Memoirs* tell us so much about the military culture of the second half of the sixteenth century, noted that for an officer 'glory, both at court and among women, consists of blows received and not blows given'. Steadiness under fire, of course, was necessarily the essence of courage in modern infantry war: if first the officers, and after them the men, were allowed to duck and flinch and step aside, then the marvellous order of rank and file would disintegrate and the company or battalion would become ungovernable and unmovable – and ripe for collapse and massacre. In the end the formidable self-discipline of the officer aristocrat was as essential to the working success of the new infantry tactics as the sergeant's hectoring barks and heavy stick.

At the highest levels of command the operational and strategic direction of armies by generals and princes increasingly emphasized the same management values that mattered at the tactical level: control, precision and technical innovation. Probably the most striking innovation was in the use of maps. The cartographic advances of the sixteenth century, usually most closely associated with the adventures of overseas discovery, were also of real military utility. The techniques of triangulation and celestial observation, as well as more careful draughtsmanship, created maps of sufficient accuracy to allow the detailed planning of military operations. Engraving and printing made maps more widely available as well. Army battle plans were increasingly expressed diagrammatically, drawn out to scale and used as an aid to exact reproduction with living men. Mapmaking was of course supremely useful in designing fortifications and planning siege operations.

Cartography allowed rulers to manage war from a distance, from the security of their palace war rooms. The artist Giorgio Vasari painted his master, Duke Cosimo de' Medici, bending over a table of maps and models, helping to plan the successful Hispano-Florentine joint conquest of Siena (1553–5), a pair of dividers in hand. Maps were not just useful to field commanders and engineers. In the first half of the sixteenth century, the emperor Charles V often directed his armies in person; in the second half of the century, his son Philip II managed Spain's wars from the Escorial, connected to the front by couriers, diplomats, spies – and map makers, who provided drawer after drawer of plans and charts. In 1580 Pope Gregory XIII ordered the creation of an entire Vatican gallery of giant painted wall maps showing all the

Duke Cosimo I of Tuscany plans the conquest of Siena in a painting by Giorgio Vasari, 1565. Cosimo measures out a distance on a fortress plan spread across a table. On the same table is a detailed study model of the walls and towers of Siena. Maps and models were new and effective tools that allowed, really for the first time, the accurate management of campaigns from a distance.

regions of Italy. Strolling along this gallery, Gregory and his successors could strategize their ongoing response to the Reformation. Another technical aid to generalship, popular at the time but (almost) completely discredited today, was astrology, which many Renaissance generals widely assumed could be used to manage time in a similar way to the use of cartography for managing distance and terrain.

And then there was the typical, powerful Renaissance influence of the ancient example. By the mid fifteenth century it was not exceptional for ambitious princes to read – or have read to them – the works of the classical historians. Exposure begat imitation. Francesco Sforza, a professional commander who seized the duchy of Milan in 1450, had himself pictured wearing an ancient-style suit of armour and conversing with a panel of classical martial worthies, including Hannibal, Julius Caesar and Themistocles. In the next century ancient military costume became something of a fashion, with the best Milanese armourers producing actual suits of real steel armour *alla Romana antica*. Charles V had a suit, complete with a Medusa's head as a shield boss. There were parallel fashions for Roman-style haircuts (very short), and classical given names: Hercules, Octavian, Alexander. At least a few of these names rubbed off on their bearers: perhaps the best general of the entire Renaissance was Alessandro Farnese, Duke of Parma and commander of Philip II's army in the Netherlands from 1578 to 1592. Further copying ancient ways, Renaissance rulers celebrated their victories with parades in imitation of an ancient Roman triumph. The first to do so was Alfonso of Aragon for his entry into a conquered Naples in 1443; to make this event permanent, he had the gateway to his downtown fortress, the Castello Nuovo, built as a triumphal arch. Princes and captains begged immortality in another way, with antique-style bronze equestrian sculptures, such as Verrocchio's magnificent memorial sculpture of the great Venetian captain Bartolommeo Colleoni (d. 1476).

The classical age was no mere source of props and motifs. As already noted, the infantry reformers whose work utterly revolutionized the Renaissance battlefield were guided by the examples of the ancient phalanx and legion. Among the first and most assiduously practical students of ancient warfare was the warlord Federigo da Montefeltro, Duke of Urbino (d. 1482), who won fame as a field commander and spent no small part of his mercenary profits building one of the best libraries of his generation. The Florentine bookseller and biographer Vespasiano da Bisticci admiringly compared Montefeltro to two different Roman generals, Scipio Africanus and Fabius Maximus, and

Ancient-style breastplate, probably of Milanese manufacture, c. 1550. This breastplate is the only surviving piece of what was certainly once a full suit of armour alla Romana antica, *with matching helmet and protection for shoulders and thighs. Though today in Florence and usually associated with Duke Cosimo I, it was quite possibly originally made for King Henry II of France, and worn at his coronation in 1547. Wearing such a suit of armour transformed a Renaissance prince into a living Roman general.*

explicitly connected the duke's knowledge of Latin and study of ancient history with his battlefield success. Princes and aspiring generals continued to mine the classics for strategic hints. The historian Francesco Guicciardini praised the Italian commander Prospero Colonna as 'the delayer' (after Fabius Cunctator, the cautious Roman general who outlasted Hannibal) in the context of a discussion of how strategy had become, by the 1530s, more important than feats of arms. Colonna's siege of Milan in 1525 was supposed to have been informed by Julius Caesar's ancient reduction of Alesia. Far beyond the specific application of ancient stratagems or maxims to the particular problems of a given campaign, it was the underlying sense of generalship, of field management as an art form, that inspired and influenced Renaissance commanders. Not the least artists of the Renaissance world were the military men who consciously styled themselves the Caesars of their age.

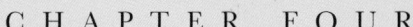

CHAPTER FOUR

Cross versus Crescent

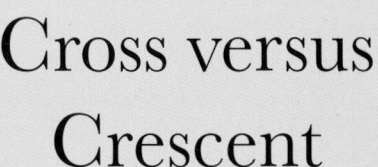

The battle of Mohacs in Hungary, 1526, a Turkish miniature from a manuscript volume of the sultan Süleyman's greatest victories. At the bottom, Ottoman light cavalry rout Hungarian horsemen, while spahi lancers on armoured horses await action. Note the sultan's bronze artillery and the infantry with firearms at centre and top left. The sultan himself, wearing a golden coat and an enormous white turban, watches his triumph unfold. At Mohacs Süleyman utterly destroyed the army of King Louis of Hungary, extinguishing one of the most important Christian kingdoms. States and princes further west feared the same fate as the Ottoman Empire pressed heavily against Christian Europe.

Cross versus Crescent

HISTORIANS, PREMATURELY ANTICIPATING the balance of power in later centuries, have largely failed to properly emphasize the Renaissance confrontation between Christian West and Muslim East. Contemporary Europeans harboured no doubts. For them war with the infidel was no sideshow or frontier skirmish but the most important struggle of all, the one fight that was clearly legitimate in the eyes of God – and the one war that had to be won. The adjacent Muslim powers, above all the Ottoman sultan, but also the sultan of Egypt, the sharif of Morocco and the pirate princelings of the North African Maghreb, agreed: war against Christendom was a duty. Both sides in the conflict were dedicated to success – and both sides had every reason to fear, or expect, eventual victory for Islam. Later generations of Europeans, from the seventeenth century on, would grow increasingly confident, even complacent, regarding their military superiority over the East (excepting such scares as the 1683 siege of Vienna). There was no such confidence in the fifteenth and sixteenth centuries. Then, a long string of battlefield victories indicated that the Muslim world, particularly the wealthy, populous, militant and expanding Ottoman Empire, had every chance of stretching its grasp to seize first Sicily or Vienna, then Naples and Rome, and finally all of western Europe. This was by no means an improbable, or even unlikely scenario. The sultan planned for it, sending his armies and fleets west. In response, the European powers fretted, drew themselves together in a sequence of Holy Leagues and prepared for the sultan's blows. Only the most powerful of Christian princes, 'his most Catholic majesty' the King of Spain, could direct his own sustained offensive east to match and meet the Turk.

The battles of East versus West were of course fought along the shores of the Mediterranean and the banks of the Danube. But there were more exotic, farther-flung points of conflict as well: the Renaissance struggle between Muslim and Christian European was the first truly global war. Portuguese exploration into the Indian Ocean in search of pepper, cloves and nutmeg (and also the fabled Eastern ally for the war against the Moors, 'Prester John', eventually identified as the black Christian king of the Ethiopian highlands) brought the age-old conflict of crusader and Ghazi to the monsoon-lands of Asia and East Africa. In 1498 Vasco da Gama made landfall in India. The Portuguese governors 'of India' (their brief actually included the whole of the Indian Ocean) who followed da Gama brought the customs of the Iberian Reconquista – fire and sword – to the work of carving out a maritime empire: this was no mere commercial creation. Afonso da Albuqerque seized Hormuz in 1509, Goa in 1510 and Malacca on the Malay Peninsula – gateway to the spice wealth of the East Indies – in 1511. These were all Muslim cities. Between 1503 and 1513 the Portuguese almost annually raided into the Red Sea; in 1517 they almost seized Jiddah, the very port of Mecca. The Mameluke sultan in Cairo (until 1517) and thereafter the Ottoman sultan had to respond to these provocations. In 1508 a Mameluke fleet co-operating with Indian Muslim rulers surprised the Portuguese at Chaul off the coast of India, but this Muslim-allied fleet was destroyed the following year. In 1538 a large Ottoman army landed at Diu in India, but failed to take the Portuguese city despite the support of a massive siege battery of 130 guns. In 1552 the

A German woodcut of Turkish cavalry with a captive Christian family, bound for the slave market. The war between Islam and Christendom was fought at two levels: there was the grand campaigning of sultans, kings and emperors, but also a constant, often undeclared conflict of raids and counter-raids, both at sea and on land. Slaves were valuable booty, and not just for Muslim raiders.

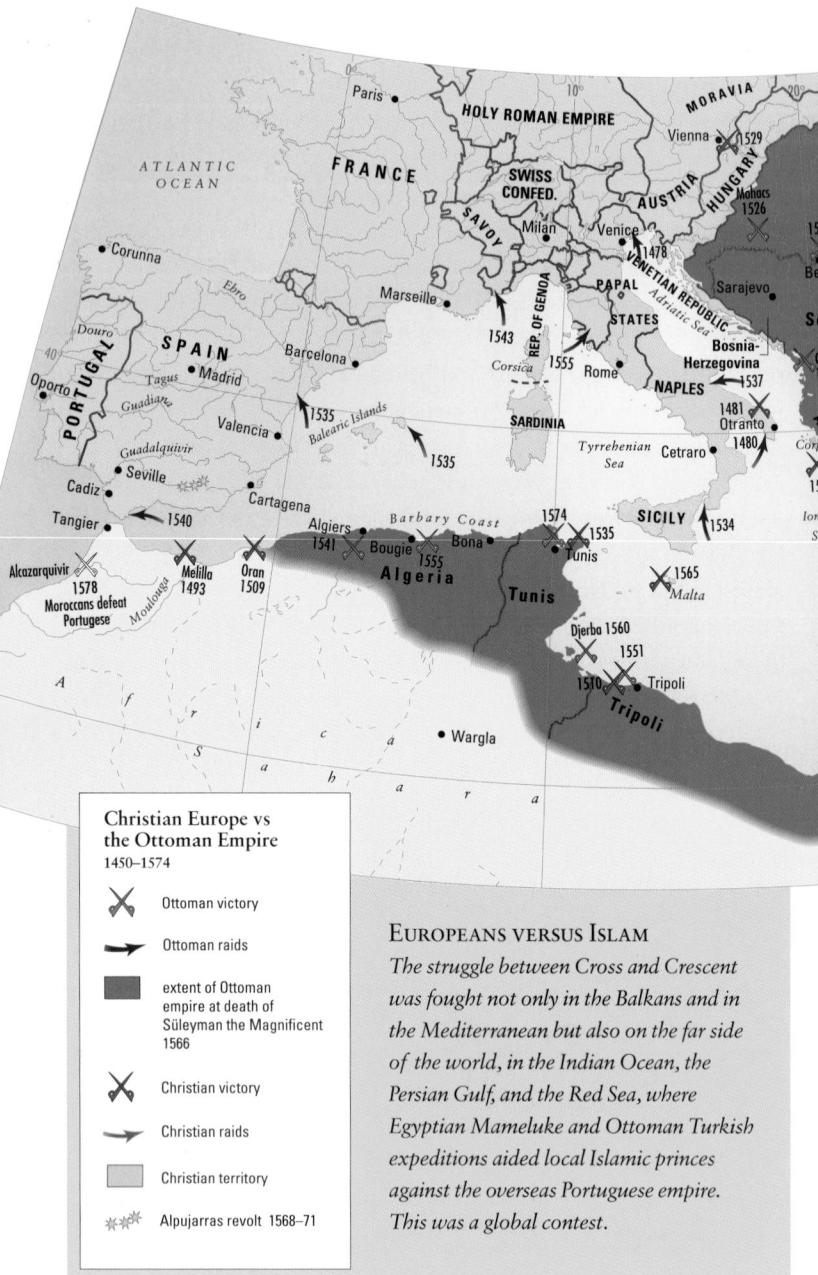

Christian Europe vs the Ottoman Empire 1450–1574

✗ Ottoman victory

➤ Ottoman raids

extent of Ottoman empire at death of Süleyman the Magnificent 1566

✗ Christian victory

➤ Christian raids

Christian territory

✱✱✱ Alpujarras revolt 1568–71

EUROPEANS VERSUS ISLAM

The struggle between Cross and Crescent was fought not only in the Balkans and in the Mediterranean but also on the far side of the world, in the Indian Ocean, the Persian Gulf, and the Red Sea, where Egyptian Mameluke and Ottoman Turkish expeditions aided local Islamic princes against the overseas Portuguese empire. This was a global contest.

Map labels:
Paris · HOLY ROMAN EMPIRE · MORAVIA · Vienna 1529 · FRANCE · AUSTRIA · HUNGARY · Mohacs 1526 · 1521 · SWISS CONFED. · SAVOY · Milan · Venice · VENETIAN REPUBLIC · Sarajevo · Belgra · ATLANTIC OCEAN · Corunna · Marseille · PAPAL STATES · Serb · Adriatic Sea · Ebro · 1478 · Bosnia-Herzegovina · Douro · SPAIN · Barcelona · Corsica 1543 1555 Rome · NAPLES 1537 · Castel 1539 · Oporto · PORTUGAL · Tagus · Madrid · Guadiana · 1535 · Balearic Islands · SARDINIA · 1481 Otranto · Alba · Valencia · 1480 Cetraro · Corfu · Guadalquivir · Cadiz · Cartagena · 1535 · Tyrrhenian Sea · 1537 · Seville · Tangier · 1540 · Barbary Coast · 1574 · SICILY 1534 · Ionian Sea · Algiers 1541 · Bougie 1555 · Bona 1535 · Tunis · 1565 Malta · Alcazarquivir 1578 Moroccans defeat Portugese · Melilla 1493 · Oran 1509 · Algeria · Tunis · Moulouya · Djerba 1560 · 1551 · 1510 Tripoli · Wargla · Tripoli · Sahara · C

126

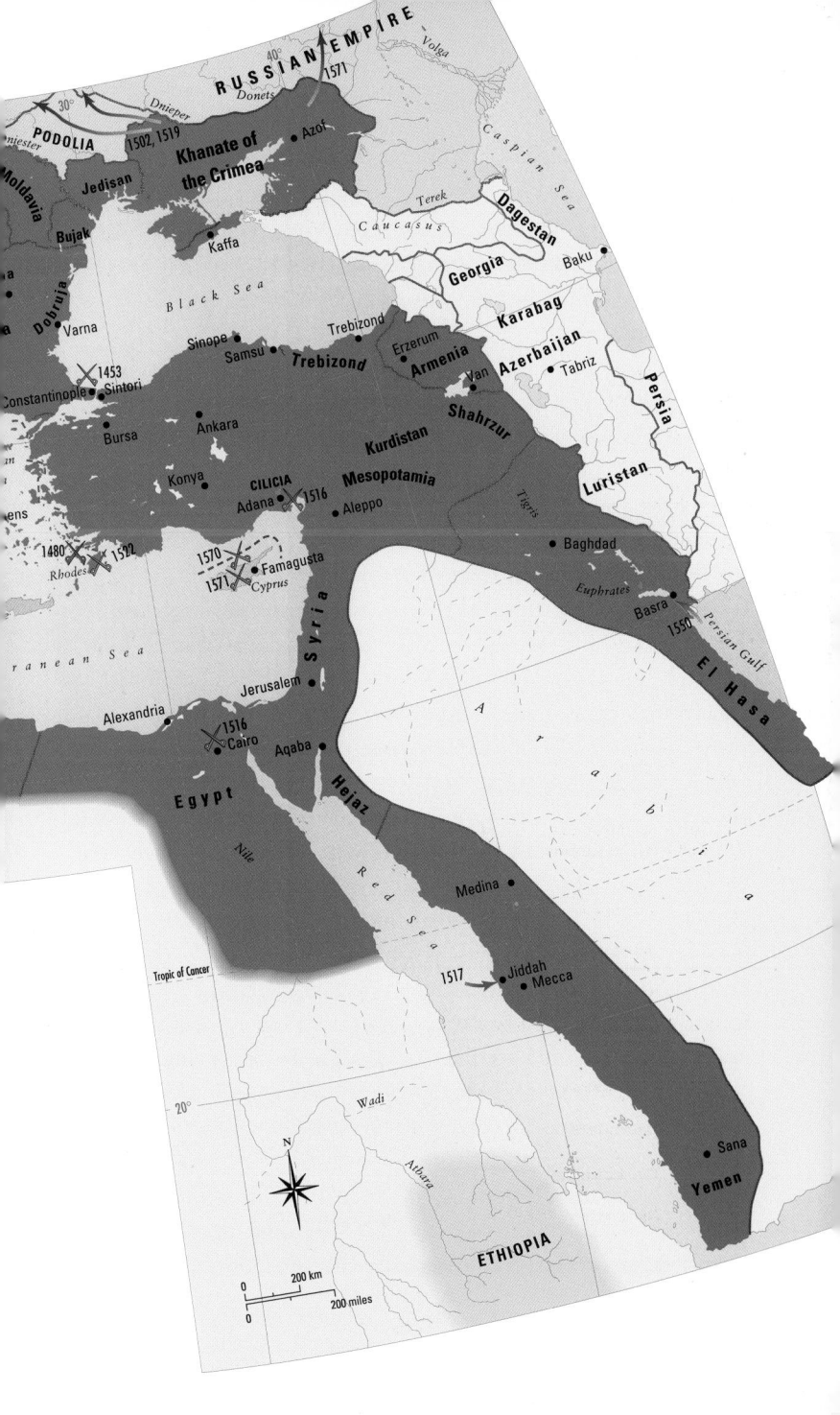

Ottomans attacked but failed to retake Hormuz; Portuguese counter-raids reached Basra in southern Iraq. In 1567 as many as forty Ottoman ships arrived at Sumatra to aid the Muslim sultan of Atjeh. Significantly this expedition coincided exactly with a peak in Ottoman activity against the Christian powers in the Mediterranean. This was indeed a world war.

In the later sixteenth century the clash between Christian and Muslim increasingly became a contest between the two most powerful princely families of the greater Mediterranean region, the Ottoman sultan in his Topkapi palace in Constantinople, and the Habsburg King of Spain in Toledo or Madrid. This struggle reached its climax in the 1560s and 1570s. There was no final military victory for either side, the real result being a stalemate that in many ways still defines the geographic frontier across the Balkans and the Mediterranean between the Christian and Muslim worlds (that religious frontier is only disintegrating today, in the early twenty-first century). But though the Renaissance conflict of Cross versus Crescent was an operational stalemate, it was none the less, all things considered, a political victory for Christendom. Outlying areas were lost – particularly by Venice – but the core lands of Western Europe remained untouched. (And, of course, European overseas expansion went substantially unchecked.) Of the important European states so gravely threatened by the Ottoman advance, only the kingdom of Hungary was extinguished. Behind this defensive success was the fact that Europe's new way of war – bastioned fortifications, scientific gunnery, disciplined infantry tactics – amounted to a battlefield revolution. This revolution was not enough – yet – to roll back the Ottoman Empire, but that time would come. The eventual long-standing military advantage of West over East was the most important long-term consequence of the Renaissance reinvention of warfare.

For most western Europeans, the first truly threatening Ottoman victory was the fall of Constantinople to Mehmed II 'the Conqueror' in 1453. This was no surprise achievement. For decades it had been clear that the Ottoman Turks were on the verge of taking Constantinople: the city was impoverished and underpopulated, an enclave completely surrounded by Ottoman territory. Generations of Byzantine envoys had begged for aid, mostly in vain. Only the still impressive ancient walls of the city kept the sultan at bay. But for his 1453 campaign Mehmed had an impressive new corps of artillery specialists, most of them Hungarians and other European renegades. From his headquarters at Edirne he dragged an artillery train of over seventy large pieces, and his gunfounders cast or forged other great bombards on the spot. In the middle of the fifteenth century there was no technical or technological gap between East and West. The sultan's cannon were soon booming away at the walls of the city: within days the great towers of Byzantium began to tumble. Meanwhile the defenders were hard-pressed to find the men to line the walls. On 29 May 1453, after only two months of siege, the exhausted, thousand-year-old capital of the Roman Empire finally fell.

Refugees from the fall brought to the West their eyewitness testimonies to the size and new power of the sultan's army. The perceived threat was enough to help encourage a formal, negotiated system of alliance among the squabbling princes and republics of Italy, who realized that they were themselves now one decisive step closer to an eventual confrontation with Mehmed. Over the next twenty-five years further westward conquests (the Morea by 1460, Bosnia in 1464, Albania in 1468) and the audacity of Turkish land raiders (in 1478 they ravaged Friuli in north-eastern Italy) underlined the threat. The long-feared direct blow came in 1480. In that year the aged 'Conqueror' launched two great attacks on western Christian territory, one against Rhodes, the island fortress of the piratical knights of St John, or knights Hospitallers, and one against the city of Otranto at the heel of Italy, in the territory of the King of Naples. Mehmed's siege of Rhodes followed the plan used at Constantinople, with a massed battery beating down the medieval walls of the city. But the doughty Hospitallers defended every breach with tenacity, and in a counter-attack following a nearly

THE SIEGE OF RHODES

The epic five-month siege of Rhodes was one of the first great victories of sultan Süleyman's long reign. His great-grandfather Mehmed 'the Conqueror' had failed to take the city in 1480 – Süleyman's success in 1522 signalled the maturing power of a now vastly larger and richer Ottoman Empire.

St Nicholas Tower

BALLAGHA AND HIS JANISSARIES

FRANCE

St Paul Gate
Trébuc Tower

GERMANY

Grand Master's Palace ④

Amboise Gate

⑦

Naval dockya

COLLACHIUM

Arsenal

St Anthony Gate

St George Gate-Tower

AUVERGNE

gate

sea gat

⑥

Tower of Spain

Trading quarters

CITY

AYASLACHA

SPAIN

Tower of the Virgin
St Athanasios Gate

AGIMED PACHA

ENGLAND

②

QASI

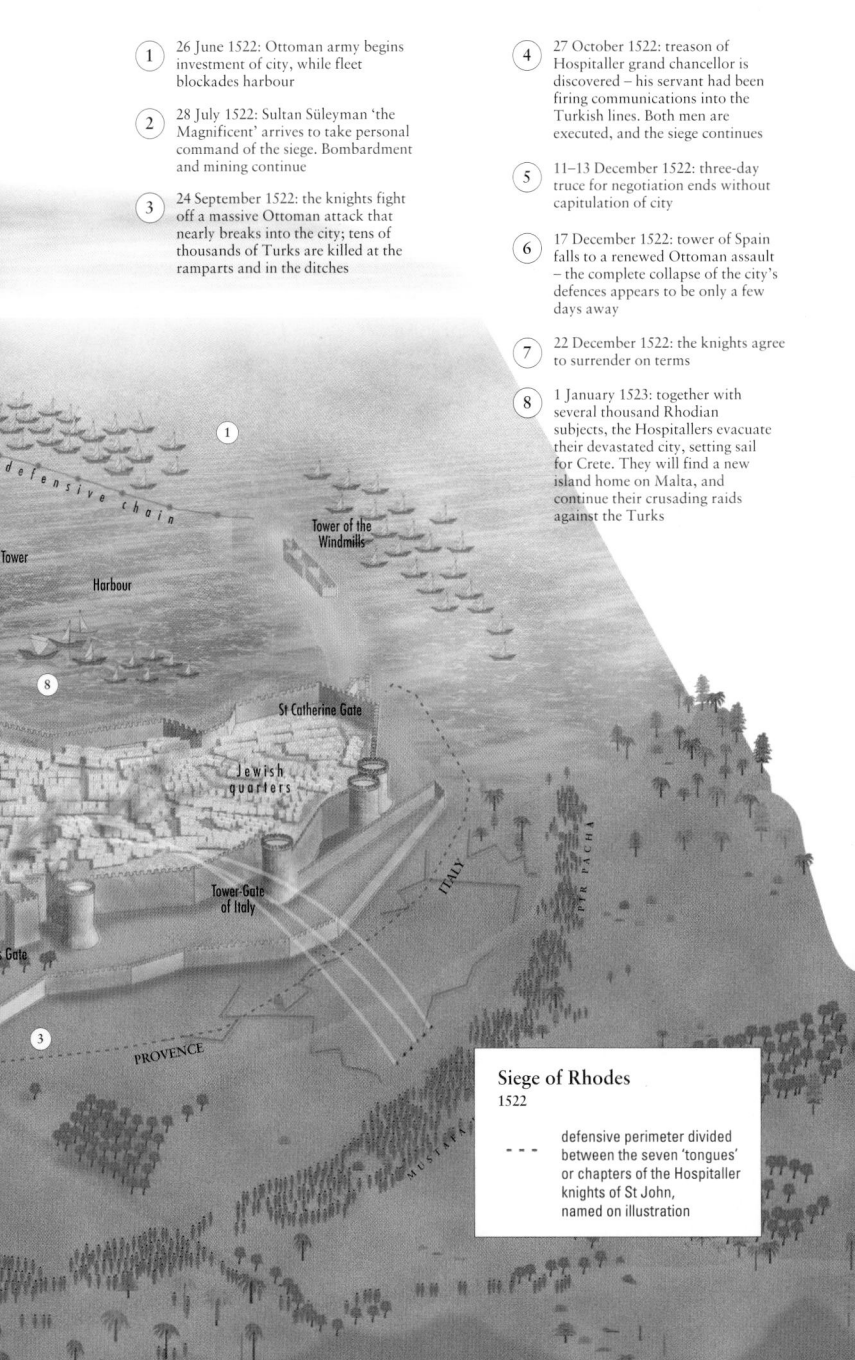

1. 26 June 1522: Ottoman army begins investment of city, while fleet blockades harbour

2. 28 July 1522: Sultan Süleyman 'the Magnificent' arrives to take personal command of the siege. Bombardment and mining continue

3. 24 September 1522: the knights fight off a massive Ottoman attack that nearly breaks into the city; tens of thousands of Turks are killed at the ramparts and in the ditches

4. 27 October 1522: treason of Hospitaller grand chancellor is discovered – his servant had been firing communications into the Turkish lines. Both men are executed, and the siege continues

5. 11–13 December 1522: three-day truce for negotiation ends without capitulation of city

6. 17 December 1522: tower of Spain falls to a renewed Ottoman assault – the complete collapse of the city's defences appears to be only a few days away

7. 22 December 1522: the knights agree to surrender on terms

8. 1 January 1523: together with several thousand Rhodian subjects, the Hospitallers evacuate their devastated city, setting sail for Crete. They will find a new island home on Malta, and continue their crusading raids against the Turks

defensive chain

Tower of the Windmills

ic Tower

Harbour

St Catherine Gate

Jewish quarters

Tower-Gate of Italy

us Gate

ITALY

PIER PACHA

PROVENCE

MUSTAFA

Siege of Rhodes
1522

- - - defensive perimeter divided between the seven 'tongues' or chapters of the Hospitaller knights of St John, named on illustration

successful assault the knights slaughtered thousands in the Turkish camp and even seized the Holy Standard of Islam from the tent of the Turkish commander. The siege had to be lifted.

Almost forgotten today is Mehmed's simultaneous amphibious attack against Otranto, though in western Europe the Ottoman assault was easily the most electric news of the year. In August 1480 about 10,000 Turkish troops landed, a large force at the time, and they easily took the small city after a brief, three-day siege. The seizure was only the opening operation of a larger intended conquest of Italy. Realizing full well the danger at hand, all the Italian states rallied to the defence of Christendom (except Venice, whose commercial connections in the East were always a complication), pledged themselves to a formal Holy Alliance against the Turk and sent money and men to help the King of Naples remove the Turkish bridgehead. Through the winter of 1480 and into the following year the allied Italian force maintained a blockade, but the decisive event of the siege occurred back in Constantinople – the sultan's death in May 1481. The resulting concentration of political energy on the capital eliminated the possibility of reinforcing Otranto, and so in September the Turkish garrison surrendered on terms (they were none the less put to death in revenge for the thousands of Christian captives massacred or sold into slavery). Many Europeans had not expected a Turkish defeat. Sensing a looming tragedy, during the siege a German cleric had made his pilgrimage to 'the Eternal City before ... it was taken by the Turks'. In 1481 the fall of Rome to the sultan was scarcely less imaginable than had been the fall of the second Rome, Constantinople, twenty-eight years before. Over the next generation, wild rumours and prophecies flourished in Italy and Europe: that the Pope had been seized by Barbary pirates, or that the sultan would take Rome, but turn Christian and usher in the next age.

With Mehmed's death Europe won a respite from substantial Ottoman attack for an entire generation. His immediate successor, Bayezid II, had to face civil war, court intrigues and internal revolt. He added little new territory to his empire. Bayezid's successor Selim was again a great warrior, but he chose to focus his energies against fellow Islamic foes. In a pair of remarkable lightning campaigns against the Mamelukes, in 1516 Selim took Syria, and in the following year he took Egypt as well, ending the Mameluke sultanate. The Ottomans were now the most powerful state in the Muslim world – in 1520 Selim's successor Süleyman II, soon to be styled 'the Magnificent' in the West for his wealth and power, inherited an empire that was vastly larger and richer than that of his great-grandfather, Mehmed the Conqueror. And Süleyman once again directed Ottoman ambitions westward. But the West had meanwhile gained a crucial respite, and at exactly the right time. The period between 1481 and 1529 (Süleyman's siege of Vienna) was exactly that time of experiment when Europe's military reformers developed the new fortifications and infantry tactics that were so critical to the Renaissance reinvention of warfare. As a result, though Süleyman brought the resources of a hugely enlarged Ottoman empire to the battlefield, the European armies he faced from 1529 on were vastly more sophisticated than those of the late fifteenth and earlier sixteenth century. Thus the European art of war caught up to the Ottoman threat at just the right moment. It was the breathing space between 1481 and the late 1520s that saved the West (or at least Austria and probably Italy), and allowed the full development of the military techniques that became a critical advantage in later European wars against the Ottoman sultan and other non-Europeans.

In 1522 the young Süleyman turned to the unfinished business of Rhodes. The knights had suffered not only the first Ottoman siege but a devastating earthquake in the following year (1481). But three successive Grand Masters of the order had dedicated themselves to modernizing the fortifications of the city. There were as yet no real angle bastions, but reinforced walls and immensely thick artillery towers had completely remade the city's defences. Süleyman's resources and resolve would have to be on an epic scale. They were. If sources can be believed the invasion fleet was of almost 300 vessels, and they landed more than 100,000 fighting troops, including 10,000 janissaries – the sultan's crack infantry

– and also 60,000 pioneers to dig mines and assault trenches. This was a far more massive enterprise than the siege of 1480. But sustained bombardment only gradually cracked the new, more powerful towers and walls; and multiple assaults only filled the ditches with Turkish dead. Yet as long as the sultan remained determined there was no chance of outside relief. With no other option besides eventual starvation, the Grand Master agreed to terms and the knights evacuated Rhodes on 1 January 1523. Süleyman honourably kept the bargain. Operationally and politically this was a tremendous victory for the sultan, but the length of this second siege – five months – and its negotiated settlement suggests that already a European investment in fortifications technique was yielding a critical tactical advantage.

After Rhodes Süleyman aimed at Hungary. Belgrade, the key fortress blocking penetration up the Danube, had already fallen in 1521. The following decade was the high-water mark of Turkish land power against the West. Süleyman's army was an interesting, balanced mix of nomad tradition and Ottoman cross-cultural innovation. Ottoman attention to the power of artillery, so precocious in the 1450s, had never waned. Süleyman went to war with enormous numbers of both field and siege guns. The sultan also had a dedicated corps of infantry, the janissaries (literally 'new troops'). These were recruited by the devshirme, a tax of sons levied on Christian rural households, particularly in the Balkans. Likely lads were taken from their families and raised in barracks in Constantinople. There they learned Turkish and how to handle weapons, especially the powerful Eastern composite bow (cunningly made of wood, sinew and horn) but also the arquebus. Through the first third of the sixteenth century the janissary corps probably had a higher proportion of men with firearms than in almost any western European army. In comparison with the West, considerably more official attention was paid to perfecting marksmanship, but there was little or no formation drill – at least as a European sergeant would have understood it. Apprentice janissaries were also taught the tenets of Islam, and they universally professed a vigorous, heterodox Muslim

The Ottoman Army besieges Belgrade in 1521, a Turkish miniature painting. Note the earth-filled timber cribs protecting the Ottoman siege guns at the centre and left. In the 1520s the sultan Süleyman's artillery was as powerful and as numerous as that of any Western king. Many of his cannon founders and artillerists were renegades from Western Europe. Belgrade's fall in 1521 opened the way for further Ottoman campaigns up the Danube and into central Europe.

faith heavily influenced by Dervish teachings and various folk beliefs, some of them patently Christian. Technically janissaries were the sultan's personal slaves (not necessarily a demeaning status), and they were not allowed to marry until retirement. They were fanatically devoted to the person of the sultan, rather than to the Ottoman state, and they could cause considerable political trouble during an interregnum, often selecting a favourite prince as the successor. Their military tactics were disciplined and leaned towards the defensive. On the battlefield they often fought in and around their wagons, which could also carry small artillery pieces. These techniques perfectly complemented the fast-moving light cavalry that made up the bulk of an Ottoman army.

Individually the janissaries were as skilled and as courageous as any western European infantry. Their reputation spread wide – Christendom well knew the calibre of the sultan's best infantry. In Naples the boys

Ottoman janissary infantry, a detail from a sixteenth-century Turkish miniature. Janissary training was very different from that of Western infantry, with little or no formation drill but strong emphasis on marksmanship. The distinctive janissary clothing and headgear owed more to late Byzantine military costume than traditional Turkic dress.

produced by the liaison of Spanish garrison soldiers and local Italian girls – sons bound to enter their fathers' companies – were nicknamed 'janissaries'. There was a crucial difference in soldiering between these namesakes destined to 'trail a pike' in a Spanish tercio, and the real thing, the janissaries of the sultan. Though ferocious warriors, the janissaries never adopted the pike or any other weapon that demanded cohesive action, and they consequently had nothing like the ordered drill of the new-style European pike and shot battalions. It is just possible that Süleyman himself understood this lack to be a weakness. According to Brantôme, Süleyman specifically recruited experienced infantry captains from the French Army in North Italy, probably in the 1530s (when sultan and French king were happily allied against Habsburg Spain). Was Süleyman just looking for a few more brave renegades – or was he seeking to reform the janissary corps on the model of the new infantry tactics of the West? In light of this latter possibility, it is fascinating to note that despite the presence of tens of thousands of experienced European veterans in all the major Mediterranean Muslim armies – in the army of the sharif of Morocco as well as that of the Turk – there is no evidence that any of the new tactics of the West ever entered an army of the East. Weapons technology spread, but not tactical technique. Assuming innovation was desired, the only conclusion possible is that the cultural barriers were simply too high for transmission to take place. This conclusion is reinforced by the record of later European experts hired to reform the Ottoman Army in the eighteenth and nineteenth centuries, who found it almost impossible to enforce changes that went against the cultural grain.

The sultan's artillery and janissaries were both impressive, but the real soul of Süleyman's army resided in the cavalry. Like the nobles of the West, the Ottoman political and military aristocracy was a horse culture. The Turkish horseman of the fifteenth and sixteenth century had given up some of the more curious details of his nomadic heritage – such as a kind of lariat used to entangle the legs of an enemy horse – but the deeper spirit of the steppe lived on. Fighting was the province of warriors, and a combination of horsemanship and athletic skill at arms (especially archery) was the quintessence of being a warrior. Ottoman cavalry, both Turkish and other ethnic types, understood discipline in the sense of courage and devotion, but not in the sense of sophisticated formal tactics. This was not necessarily a detriment. After all, Eastern horse, in the form of stradiots, hussars and others, were in high demand in the armies of the West. But these light horse were a small proportion of any Venetian, French or Spanish army, and they were supplementary hirelings – not the core and political élite. Turkish noble cavalry, the spahis, took the field in enormous numbers, and were usually the largest portion of the regular field army. (There were always large swarms of irregular horse and foot as well.)

The spahis were not just the core of the sultan's army, they were also representatives and products of one of the defining institutions of the Ottoman Empire, the timar system. Each horseman was supported by a particular piece of land, a timar, which was not a fief but a gift for life from the sultan. The spahi's equipment depended on the quality of that holding. Probably only the wealthiest had complete suits of mail armour, reinforced with attached plates; most had only a helmet and a mail shirt. Their horses, though light in comparison with those of a western man-at-arms or pistoleer, were excellent. The weapons of choice remained the light lance, the scimitar and, above all, the bow. Again, we have evidence of cultural resistance to change. Like many a Christian prince, Süleyman was personally fascinated by pistols, as were other well-placed Ottomans. According to a Habsburg ambassador, at mid sixteenth century a Turkish prince attempted to rearm his personal retinue with firearms, but the horsemen refused to have anything to do with the weapons and so the attempted innovation, fascinatingly similar to contemporary cavalry experiments in western Europe, was a failure. Aristocratic distaste for firearms was also present in the West, but there it was a minority and reactionary sentiment. This was not so in Ottoman lands, where janissary slave soldiers adopted the new weapons, but the landed nobility remained aloof.

In 1526 Süleyman invaded Hungary with an army at least 70,000 fighting men strong, including some 35,000 spahis and 15,000 janissaries. Various lesser cavalry and infantry made up the rest, and there was a second army of camp followers and pack animals. The Hungarian Army under King Louis was much smaller, around 24,000 men, including some 4,000 men-at-arms. The two forces met at Mohacs. Though outnumbered, the Hungarians chose to act aggressively. The heavily armoured Hungarian men-at-arms easily charged through the outer lines of Turkish light cavalry – the knights may indeed have been deliberately drawn forward – but then they came up against a strong defensive position of infantry, wagons and guns. Caught against this obstacle, the Hungarian men-at-arms were annihilated by the massed fire of the sultan's janissaries and artillery. The Hungarians who survived to flee were easily run down by the Turkish horse – few besides light hussars escaped with their lives. It was a signal military disaster for Christendom that ended, in a day, the once-great medieval kingdom of Hungary, and it moved the frontiers of the Ottoman Empire directly against that of the Habsburgs.

Significantly, at Mohacs the Ottoman Army was better equipped with firearms than its Christian opponents, and the Turks showed better skill at co-ordinating cavalry with cannon and infantry – thanks to their wagon laager, a tactic learned during previous Hungarian wars. To add to this irony, the Hungarians at Mohacs had considered awaiting the sultan's attack behind their own wagon defence, but the knightly nobility had instead insisted on a glorious charge.

Three years after Mohacs Süleyman arrived before Vienna, ready to continue his conquests into the heart of Europe. Vienna was the capital of Archduke Ferdinand of Austria, brother to Emperor Charles V; this was the Habsburg homeland. The sultan's army was his usual immense force; the Viennese garrison a mixture of the city militia and German, Spanish and other professional soldiers, perhaps 20,000 in total. The defenders included hundreds of veterans experienced in the progessive siegecraft of the Italian wars; many of the infantry were armed with the arquebus, and practised in its use. Unlike Mohacs, at Vienna the Turks had no technical or technological advantage. Defensive preparations for the siege were in the best modern fashion. The suburbs of the city were brutally razed, and the existing medieval walls heaped with earth from behind to strengthen them. New lines of supporting ditches were dug behind the weakest lengths of rampart. The Ottoman siege works concentrated against a gate on the south-east front of the city, actually one of the few gates guarded by a modern artillery tower. Süleyman invested the city in the last week of September – dangerously late in the season. There was not much time for extended mining and serious battery, and it seems that the janissaries and other assault troops were ordered forward prematurely, attacking too-narrow breaches. Meanwhile the defenders made several aggressive sorties in force, causing substantial casualties and disrupting siege work (but suffering significant losses as well). After a series of failed assaults, on 14 October Süleyman lifted the siege; it had lasted only six weeks. The rains of autumn had already begun, and the retreat south and east along boggy roads was a nightmare. Thousands perished from hunger, exposure and

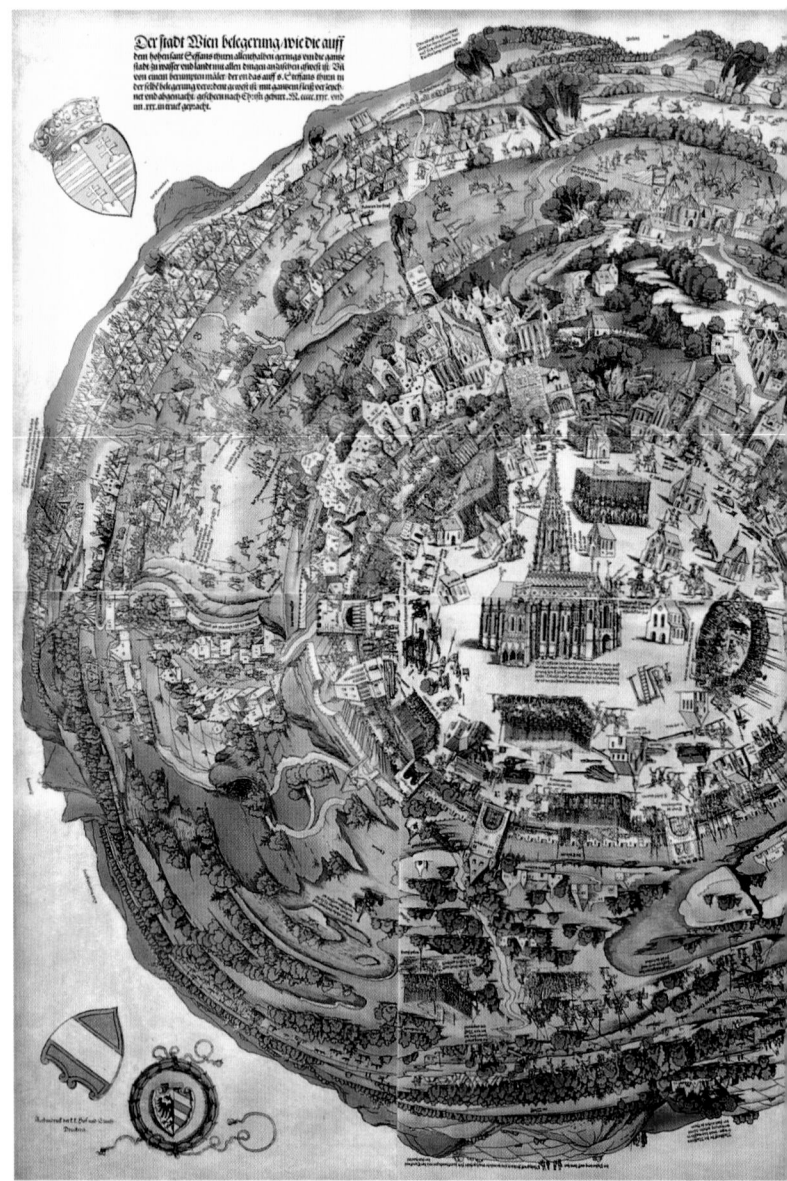

harassing cavalry. Süleyman would never again dare to attack Vienna directly.

After the setback at Vienna and an indecisive campaign against Austria in 1532, Süleyman concentrated his western ambitions on the Mediterranean front. Here his main adversary was again Emperor Charles V, who had his own dreams of expanding his empire. By inheritance Charles was Lord of Spain, Sicily, Naples, Burgundy, the Netherlands and the Holy Roman Empire, a nominal title that did include some real power. His armies had won him the rich duchy of Milan in Europe, and in the Americas Cortes had conquered Mexico (1521) and Pizarro, Peru (1533). In time the enormous silver wealth of these New World possessions would help finance the Habsburg war effort against the sultan. In sum, the King of Spain was the only Christian prince with the manpower and treasure to confront Süleyman. Charles had inherited more than land. Two of his grandparents were Ferdinand of Aragon and Isabella of Castile, the monarchs whose marriage created modern Spain, and who had expelled the last Muslim principality in Iberia, the Nasrid kingdom of

A remarkable 360 degree panoramic view of the 1529 Ottoman siege of Vienna, a composite of six woodcut prints. The successful defence of Vienna finally blocked the sultan Süleyman's advance up the Danube, an advance that began with the fall of Belgrade in 1521. Had Vienna fallen, southern Germany and northern Italy would both have been ripe for invasion.

Granada. The Reconquest had come to an end in 1492, but the war against the Moor had continued nevertheless – now it was prolonged overseas. In North Africa Spain seized Melilla (1493), Oran and Mers-el-kebir (1509) and Tripoli in Libya (1510). War against the infidel was Charles's heritage, and when he became King of Spain in 1516 he became the leader of an ongoing crusade. It was an obligation his 'most Catholic majesty' took very seriously.

The Ottoman threat to Europe had of course been creeping south and west exactly as Spanish power advanced eastward along the littoral of North Africa. It would be a mistake to exaggerate Spanish influence into the interior of the Maghreb. Local client princes were weak and unreliable, and Spanish garrisons, apart from an occasional exciting and lucrative raid, largely remained locked within the walls of their coastal forts, eating garbanzo beans and dreaming of home. It was hot and boring duty – a foretaste of European colonial service in centuries to come. The Ottoman sultan, especially after the conquest of Mameluke Egypt in 1517 (during the first year of King Charles's reign), enjoyed his own growing influence along the central North African coast. The sultan's most successful client was Khayr ad-Din, the Barbary pirate better known as Barbarossa for his red beard. Fearful of the growing Spanish influence which threatened his corsairing, in 1518 Barbarossa pledged himself to the sultan Selim and in return received a title and military aid. With a large galley fleet and a mixed army of Maghrebis, Christian renegades, Moorish refugees from Spain and Turkish adventurers, Khayr ad-Din seized Algiers (1529) and Tunis (1534) from local Muslim rulers. In 1533 Süleyman made the pirate his high admiral with all the substantial resources of the Galata dockyards at Constantinople. Barbarossa continued to plague the shores and shipping of Christian Europe until his death in 1546. These were not insubstantial raids, threatening only unlucky fishermen and villagers, but major acts of war. In 1543, his most spectacular year, Barbarossa first sacked Reggio Calabria (for the second time) and then, co-operating with the sultan's French allies, the city of Nice (a possession of the Spanish-allied Duke of Savoy). The war in North Africa and on the waters of the western Mediterranean thus became a confrontation between the emperor Charles and the sultan Süleyman.

In Charles's first Mediterranean offensive he personally led the great invasion fleet and 25,000-man army that sailed from Barcelona to take Tunis in 1535, a direct response to Barbarossa's seizure of the city the previous year. The fortified island of Goletta off Tunis became one of the principal Spanish forts of the Maghreb, and the southernmost position of a Habsburg cordon stretching down from Naples, Sicily and Malta to block further Ottoman expansion. Süleyman replied to the loss of Tunis with a planned invasion of Italy in 1537, landing a preliminary force of horse under the command of an Italian renegade

A horse disembarking from a Spanish transport, a detail from a drawing of the Spanish conquest of Tunis in 1535. The fall of Tunis was the Habsburg Emperor Charles V's first great blow against Ottoman power in North Africa. A similar expedition against Algiers failed miserably in 1541. As this detail indicates, the logistical complications of large-scale amphibious warfare were considerable.

to scour the countryside of Apulia. To secure his crossing to Italy Süleyman first laid siege to the Venetian fortress of Corfu, extensively protected by massive new-style fortifications. The Turkish besiegers proved incapable of reducing the Venetian citadel, and the entire operation had to be abandoned. The next year Charles continued the Spanish offensive, his Genoese admiral Andrea Doria taking Castelnuovo (now Herceg Novi) in Montenegro. In the late summer of 1539 Barbarossa retook Castelnuovo at a tremendous cost of life. Neither power could successfully bridge the straits of Otranto.

In 1541 Charles directed an enormous fleet against Algiers, a twin to his successful operation against Tunis in 1535. Again the emperor was personally in command, and success looked certain: Barbarossa was in the eastern Mediterranean; the janissary garrison tiny. But soon after

Charles V meets with the Bey of Tunis, 1535. Both Habsburg and Ottoman power in North Africa depended in part on agreements with local clients. Here the size of the Imperial expedition of 1535 is apparent. Note the lines of galleys in the bay to the upper right – projecting power across the Mediterranean took enormous resources.

disembarking a tremendous three-day gale utterly wrecked the supporting Spanish fleet, and the invading force (reduced to eating their horses) had to be evacuated. For almost ten years following this Spanish disaster there were no major land operations in the Mediterranean. Then the Ottoman advance resumed. Tripoli fell in 1551 (held since 1530 by the knights of St John) and Bougie in 1555. Heavy raids timed to support French adventures hit Tuscany, Spain's ally, in 1555 and 1557. A Spanish force was destroyed at Jerba on the North African coast in 1560, and the Spanish fleet was again wrecked by storm in 1562, this time off Valencia. Advantage seemed to be passing to the Turk.

Süleyman's next great blow fell against Malta in 1565. Charles had given the island to the Hospitallers, homeless again after the loss of Tripoli. One of their first acts after taking possession of the island in 1552 – by now they were experts in such things – was to commission a survey of the island's defences by a progressive Italian architect. The result of his recommendations was a new star-patterned fort, St Elmo, and several angled bastions built to take full advantage of every possibility for flanking fire. The island's defences were state of the art. Süleyman's 200-ship armada landed in May, and within a week a force of perhaps 40,000 men – an incredible number for an amphibious operation – had begun to pound the fortress of St Elmo and the town of Birgu. Reduced to rubble, St Elmo fell in late June, but Birgu held on and Turkish losses mounted, every stratagem failing, including a massive wooden wheeled tower that was blasted apart by point-blank cannon fire. In early August Hospitaller cavalry, based elsewhere on the island (and foolishly left in peace), swooped down on the Turkish camp, massacring the sick and the wounded. Later that month the Turks learned that a critical supply ship had been captured en route. On 6 September a Spanish relief fleet from Sicily unloaded 16,000 men. Exhausted and facing disaster, two days later the Turks began to evacuate; thousands were cut down during a difficult retreat and re-embarkation. The north–south Habsburg cordon across the central Mediterranean had held.

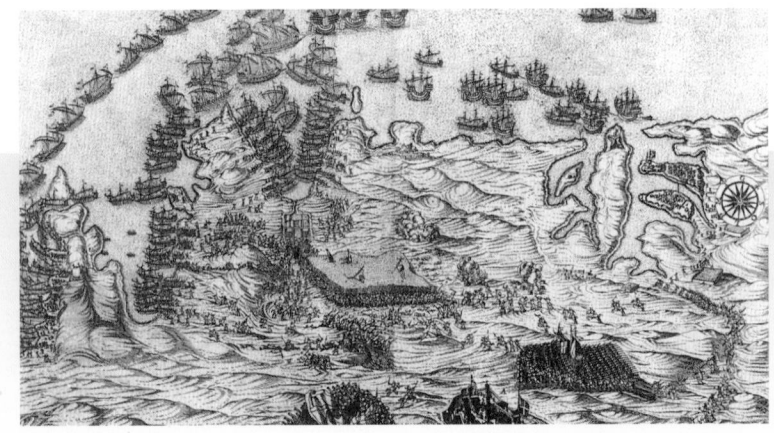

A sixteenth-century engraving of the defeated Ottoman Army re-embarking to evacuate Malta in September 1565. At the right of this print are the main harbour and fortifications of the island, rotated 90 degrees counter-clockwise from the map view below.

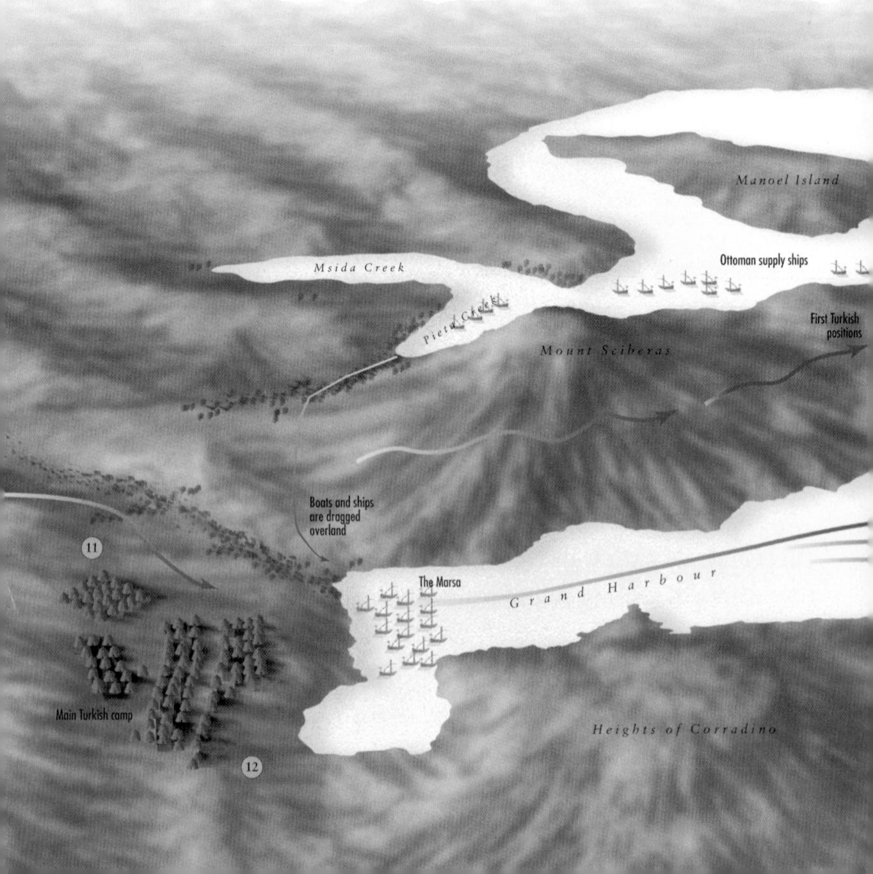

Manoel Island

Ottoman supply ships

Msida Creek

First Turkish positions

Pietà Creek

Mount Sciberas

Boats and ships are dragged overland

11

The Marsa

Grand Harbour

Main Turkish camp

12

Heights of Corradino

THE SIEGE OF MALTA

In significance the failed Ottoman siege of Malta in 1565 was a twin to the failed siege of Vienna in 1529. Malta would have given the sultan a perfect staging area for further amphibious attacks against Sicily, Italy and even Spain – a staging area free of the political complications of North Africa.

1 24 May: Turkish guns begin their bombardment of Fort St Elmo

2 6 June: new Ottoman artillery positions increase fire against Fort St Elmo

3 6 June: Turkish assault seizes outer ravelin of St Elmo fortress

4 19 June: the knights re-emplace artillery to better fire on the Ottoman positions on Mount Sciberas

5 23 June: Ottoman assault on Fort St Elmo takes horrible casualties, but the isolated citadel finally falls. Within days the Turkish siege guns are remounted to bear against Fort St Angelo, across the Grand Harbour

6 15 July: Turkish assault fails to take the St Michael bastion, despite a powder explosion that damages the knights' positions

7 15 July: attempted Janissary boat attack against Senglea destroyed by cannonade from Fort St Angelo

8 2 August: beginning of continuous five-day bombardment by all Ottoman batteries

9 7 August: Turkish assault against Castile bastion is caught and destroyed between outer and inner walls

10 7 August: Turks temporarily take St Michael bastion, but a counter-attack evicts them with heavy losses

11 7 August: under cover of the general Ottoman assaults against Senglea and Birgu, a raiding party of Hospitaller cavalry torches the Ottoman camp and massacres the sick and wounded

12 8 September: their position hopeless now that a Spanish relief army from Sicily has landed on Malta, the Ottomans evacuate camp. The siege is over

Tigne

Dragut Point

Ottoman gun positions

Fort St Elmo

Gallows Point

Fort St Angelo

chain boom

Bighi Bay

Dockyard Creek

Windmills

Senglea

Pontoon bridge

Birgu town

St Michael bastion

Kalkara Creek

Castile bastion

Chain boom

Stake palisade

French Creek

Mount Salvador

Ruins of Bormula

Heights of St Margaret

Malta was the penultimate campaign of Süleyman's long, hard-fighting reign. (His arch-antagonist Emperor Charles V had retired in 1556 and died two years later, leaving Spain, Italy and the Netherlands to his son Philip and the Austrian lands, together with the title of emperor, to his brother Ferdinand.) In 1566, though 72 years old, Süleyman personally directed a campaign up the Danube, looking for glory once again. He did not find it. Distracted into besieging an out-of-the-way castle at Sziget in Habsburg-held Hungary, he died in camp. Two days later, after a siege of over a month, Sziget gave out – its final handful of defenders lit a very long fuse leading to their remaining gunpowder, and then made a suicide sortie. The powder store blew just as the castle filled with exulting Turks, killing hundreds. The day – 8 September – was the exact anniversary of the evacuation of Malta the previous year. Sziget had fallen, but the sultan was dead, the campaign year was exhausted, and once again the fortified Habsburg perimeter had held firm.

The death of Süleyman did not put an end to the long series of wars between Christendom and the Ottoman Empire. In 1570 Süleyman's successor, Selim II, reached for the Venetian island of Cyprus. Renaissance Venice had already fought the Ottomans three times before (1463–79, 1499–1502 and 1537–40), losing substantial territories in Greece. Though the Serene Republic was always prepared for war with the Turk, because of the vulnerability of her maritime empire, and for reasons of trade, her life's blood, Venice always preferred peace, even if coexistence with the sultan gave the appearance of co-operation. Around 1510 a French ambassador sulked that the Venetians were secretly dividing the world with the Turk (a generation later a desperate King of France would openly ally with Süleyman). The usually subtle Venetian diplomacy failed in 1570. That summer Selim landed an army on Cyprus which made unexpectedly short work of the walls at Nicosia, recently and expensively refortified with a perfect perimeter of model angle bastions. The siege took only seven weeks; the population was massacred or enslaved. Next was Famagusta, also robustly fortified –

Ottoman cavalry and janissary infantry march on the Hungarian frontier, 1566. Despite their finery Western commentators stressed the comparative frugality of Turkish soldiers, each of whom mixed and cooked his own gruel of flour, water and spices. Janissaries received a daily measured ration from the sultan's stores. Spahi horsemen campaigned with their own private pack animals. This was Süleyman's last campaign; he died in camp just before the fall of the fortress of Sziget.

but this was a coastal port, much more easily replenished by sea, and here the garrison held on tenaciously, the siege stretching through the winter of 1570 and into the summer of the following year. But no army of relief arrived: Venice was too weak and too far away to mount the operation herself, and too cautious to quickly agree to a Christian crusading alliance. Finally Famagusta surrendered on terms in the first week of August 1571. The terms were not kept. Instead the garrison was murdered and their commander flayed alive. Two months later the combined navies of a new Holy League (Venice, the Pope and King Philip II of Spain) trounced the sultan's fleet at Lepanto off western Greece. It was the greatest Christian naval victory of the century, but the Venetian government was more interested in restoring commerce than pursuing any crusade. In 1573 Venice agreed to a separate peace, giving

up Cyprus: the Pope was irate, but Philip II received the news from the Venetian ambassador with 'the slightest ironic movement of his mouth'.

Besides responsibility for the long crusade against the sultan Philip had inherited from his father Charles a nearer potential Islamic foe. After the Spanish conquest of Granada in 1492 the Nasrid political élite emigrated to North Africa, but most Muslims remained behind, and many of these, the Moriscos, only nominally converted to Christianity, especially in remote areas. On Christmas Day 1568 the Moriscos of the Alpujarras mountains in central Granada broke into revolt, unable to abide new laws that banned Arabic language and culture. The outbreak proved very difficult to contain or suppress, being both a civil and a guerrilla war. Both sides committed atrocities and the markets clogged with Morisco slaves. The fear at the Spanish

court – and in Rome – was that intervention from Algiers or Constantinople could make the revolt an occasion for a major invasion, even a reconquest in reverse. Ominously in 1569 the sultan requested the use of Toulon from the King of France for a naval base; a major Franco-Ottoman operation in the western Mediterranean seemed a distinct possibility. In Spain the mood was not for half-measures, and so Philip II determined on a grim solution to his internal religious frontier: a round-up of suspect Morisco communities and their mass deportation to

An allied Catholic Christian fleet of Venetian, Spanish, and Papal vessels crushes the Ottoman fleet at the battle of Lepanto on the western coast of Greece, 1571. The victory did not reverse the 1570–71 Turkish conquest of Venetian Cyprus, but did end the threat of a substantial Ottoman naval intervention into the western Mediterranean.

Castile. This was a pitiless strategy, but it worked. Spain's captain general in the Alpujarras, Philip's half-brother Don Juan, went on to glory in 1571, captaining the victorious Holy League fleet that smashed the Ottoman navy at Lepanto: the war against the infidel was fought in many ways, both grand and small.

Philip was not the only Iberian crusader king. His cousin Sebastian of Portugal dreamed of adding a North African kingdom to his empire, and in 1578 a recent civil war in Morocco gave him the opportunity. He allied with a deposed sharif and landed near Tangier with a very mixed army of Portuguese and foreign mercenary–adventurers (including a detachment of papal arquebusiers under an English Catholic, Thomas Stukeley, originally intended for Ireland). Sebastian's little army met the much larger force of Abd al-Malik, the reigning sharif of Morocco, at Alcazarquivir. The mass of al-Malik's army were traditional light horse, but he also had plenty of artillery, and a numerous and well-trained infantry armed with firearms, including thousands of renegades. The crusaders sensibly guarded their flanks with wagons but they were still overwhelmed. Sebastian was killed, his body never recovered. He left no strong heir and two years later Philip of Spain annexed Portugal with a small, sharp invasion. Philip's empire, including his new Portuguese territories overseas, now reached around the globe: he possessed some scrap of land in all twenty-four modern time zones.

Philip did not use the resources of this newly enlarged empire for a Mediterranean campaign against the sultan, even though Tunis and Goletta had fallen in 1574 (the swansong of the Ottoman fleet, which otherwise never recovered from Lepanto). War had exhausted both Mediterranean great powers. Philip had repudiated his debts in 1575 – the third bankruptcy of his reign – and in 1584 the sultan devalued his currency by over 50 per cent. Both rulers were, in a real sense, financially prostrate, and both empires faced grave internal troubles: Spain in the Netherlands, the Ottomans in North Africa. In the Mediterranean truce replaced conflict.

In a larger sense the Mediterranean calm after 1580 emphasized the contemporary obstacles to projecting force. The Ottoman Empire could tackle even the best-protected Christian cities if they were close to the empire's centre of power in the eastern Mediterranean (Nicosia and Famagusta in 1570–71, like Rhodes in 1522). Otherwise Christendom's fortified perimeter stood firm (Malta, 1565). On the other hand the new strength of the West, as compared with the period before 1529, remained defensive. Efforts to roll back earlier Ottoman conquests (a disastrous 1541 siege of Buda), or attempt dramatic new ones (Alcazarquivir, 1578), uniformly failed. Stalemate yielded a certain geopolitical clarity. In Spain the Inquisition and deportations erased internal religious boundaries. Externally an understood political frontier between Christendom and Islam now curved, with exceptions (the remaining Iberian posts in North Africa, the Venetian Empire), from the straits of Hercules to the straits of Otranto, and from there north through a divided Hungary.

A suit of armour belonging to Philip II of Spain, manufactured in Augsburg, 1552.

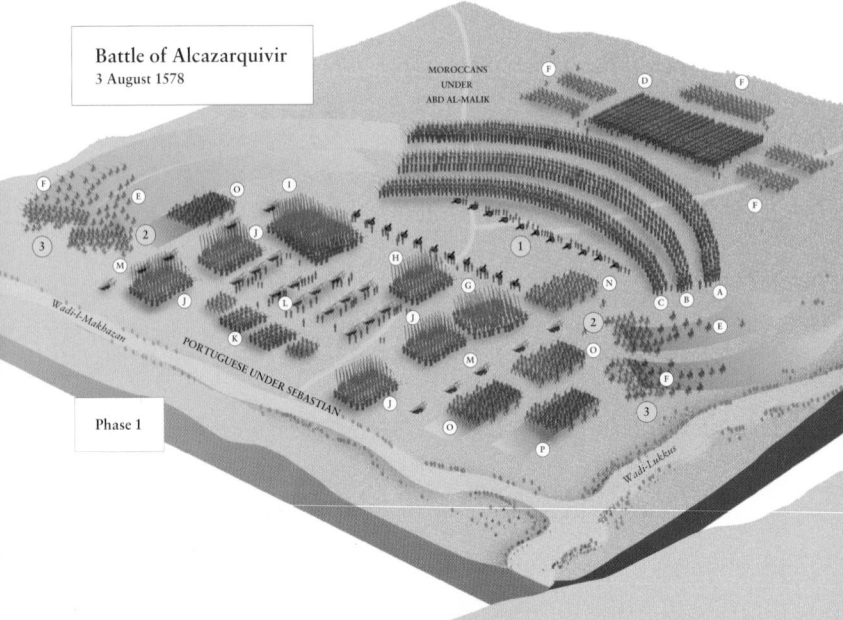

Battle of Alcazarquivir
3 August 1578

MOROCCANS
UNDER
ABD AL-MALIK

Wadi-l-Makhazan

PORTUGUESE UNDER SEBASTIAN

Phase 1

Wadi-l-Lukkus

(A) Moroccan and Turkish infantry

(B) Renegade Christian infantry

(C) Andalusi infantry

(D) Reserve infantry and guard

(E) Horse arquebusiers

(F) Light cavalry

(G) German and Walloon infantry

(H) Portuguese 'adventurer' infantry

(I) Castilian and English infantry

(J) Portuguese regular infantry

(K) Arquebusier and reserve horse

(L) Baggage and noncombatants

(M) Flanking wagons with arquebusiers

(N) Tangier veteran cavalry

(O) Portuguese heavy cavalry

(P) Allied Moroccan light horse

(1) Moroccan and Portuguese artillery exchange fire

(2) Steady fire from Moroccan horse arquebusiers disrupts Portuguese flanks

(3) Light horse begin to encircle Portuguese army

ALCAZARQUIVIR, 1578
Renaissance developments in the European art of war were not enough to overcome any operational circumstance or political folly. At Alcazarquivir a not unsophisticated Moroccan army, including thousands of renegade Turks and Christians, with firearms, annihilated the smaller crusading force from Portugal.

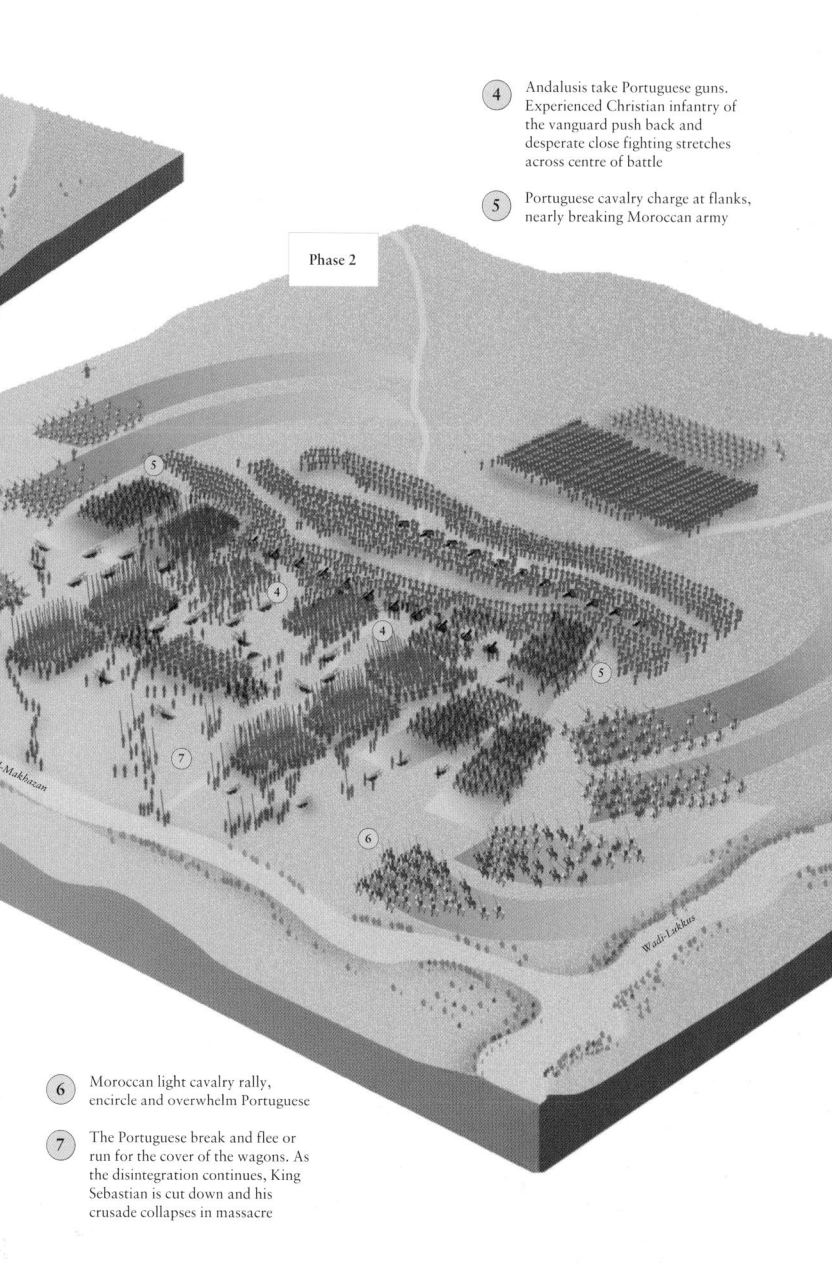

4 Andalusis take Portuguese guns. Experienced Christian infantry of the vanguard push back and desperate close fighting stretches across centre of battle

5 Portuguese cavalry charge at flanks, nearly breaking Moroccan army

Phase 2

6 Moroccan light cavalry rally, encircle and overwhelm Portuguese

7 The Portuguese break and flee or run for the cover of the wagons. As the disintegration continues, King Sebastian is cut down and his crusade collapses in massacre

CHAPTER FIVE

Duelling Kings

The death of a Swiss pikeman, a detail from the battle of Pavia (1525) tapestry series. The animosities between the princes of Renaissance Europe were often no less intense, and no less personal, than any battlefield encounter. The most consequential dynastic struggle was between the Valois kings of France and the Habsburg Holy Roman Emperors and kings of Spain. Their competition focused on two of the richest territories in Europe, the kingdom of Naples and the duchy of Milan, but it was also over something more intangible, and more precious: acknowledged primacy as the greatest ruling house in Christendom.

Duelling Kings

HIGH POLITICS IN the Renaissance meant dynastic politics. Most states (and most parts of states) were dependencies of a given family, either by ancient inheritance or by more recent gift or usurpation. There were a few exceptions to hereditary and personal rule – including the Venetian republic, the papacy and various cities and city leagues within the Holy Roman Empire – but most of these states were politically negligible (the bishopric of Liège, the republic of Lucca), and many of them were really alliances or oligarchies of competing noble factions. Perhaps only the Swiss confederacy of burghers and free peasants truly stood apart. These few and partial exceptions noted, Renaissance Europe was ruled by titled aristocrats, men and women whose political identities and instincts were familial rather than constitutional or national.

Or confessional – even amidst the flames of Reformation, dynastic concerns could trump religion. Henry VIII of England, previously an eloquent defender of the Roman church, from 1531 gradually severed his connection with the Pope once it became clear that the king's marriage to the luckless Catherine of Aragon, who had only produced a daughter, would never receive papal nullification. Henry's royal need for a son was paramount. Later in the sixteenth century, in France, Henry of Navarre three times trimmed his religious convictions for political advantage: first in 1572, when he left his Calvinist

Duelling kings
1494–1598

⚔ Habsburg victory

⚔ Habsburg defeat

— boundary of Holy Roman Empire

▮ Habsburg empire of Charles V

▮ lands of Philip II of Spain

▮ lands of the Emperor Ferdinand

DUELLING KINGS
In the first four decades of the sixteenth century the cockpit of European war was northern Italy, particularly Milan. In the 1550s, with Italy essentially settled, the northern front between France and the Empire became more important.

birth-faith after marrying a Catholic royal princess, Marguerite of Valois; then in 1576 he returned to Protestantism to lead the Huguenot party; finally, in 1593, he again abjured and accepted Catholicism in order to be crowned Henry IV of France. Although Henry's exceptional slipperiness particularly enraged the zealots – and he died under the knife of an assassin – his direct descendants ruled France until 1789.

Naturally enough, dynastic politics begat dynastic wars, and these spanned the political spectrum from high to low. Some quarrels were based on competing geneologies and overlapping claims to the same territories and titles; others rested on hate alone. At the grandest level whole kingdoms were at stake as two or more pedigreed families competed for a royal prize. In the second half of the fifteenth century the rival houses of York and Lancaster disputed the throne of England; a hundred years later, as the last of the Valois expired one by one without issue, Catholic Guise and Huguenot Bourbon – Henry of Navarre again – manoeuvred and fought for the crown of France. Dynastic struggle could be petty as well. In and around Rome an on-again, off-again private war between the Colonna and Orsini clans routinely defied the authority of the Pope. Even farther down the aristocratic food chain, in the Venetian town of Udine in north-eastern Italy, the della Torre and Savorgnano families perpetually circled one another. Their vendetta came to a head in the spring of 1511, when, inflamed by a carnival prank (a della Torre boy was caught painting his family insignia on a well head before the Savorgnano town house), the Savorgnano flew to arms and massacred their despised local enemies.

As often as not the military campaigns of Europe's great monarchs were hardly more reasonable than any backwater blood feud and certainly no less personal. In 1528 the Valois King of France, Francis I, humiliated by a long string of grave battlefield defeats, formally challenged his Habsburg rival, Emperor Charles V, to a duel that would end their competition once and for all, man against man. In 1536 Charles V – standing in St Peter's in Rome, the very centre of Christendom, and fresh from his victory over the infidel at Tunis –

surprised his audience with a sudden and stirring challenge of his own: he would face the King of France without armour, and with naked sword and dagger in hand – terms that meant a fight to the death. Charles gave Francis twenty days to respond, but the French king prevaricated, and the already decades-old Habsburg–Valois struggle went on as before, waged conventionally with armies and fleets.

Indeed, the struggle between Habsburg Spain and Valois France was the greatest dynastic confrontation of the age. It began in the very late fifteenth century when Spain, not yet a Habsburg territory, and the Habsburg emperor Maximilian I both joined the 'Holy League' (supposedly to continue against the Turk) that foiled a Valois attempt on the kingdom of Naples. Competing Spanish and French intervention in Italy continued, most action shifting to northern Italy from the early sixteenth century, with the duchy of Milan at stake. The Italian Wars peaked in the 1520s, with Spain – now the hub of Charles V's great and growing Habsburg Empire – substantially evicting France from Italy. But the Valois continued to send expeditions into the peninsula for a generation, searching for fresh revenge on old battlefields. Meanwhile, fighting also took place on northern fronts where Habsburg territories in the Netherlands and Germany abutted France, and where the continental warring provided an opportunity for the ambitions of Henry VIII of England. A defining peace only came in 1559.

This half century of open war and simmering peace was yet to come when Charles VIII, the Valois King of France, invaded Italy in 1494. Charles's immediate claim was to the kingdom of Naples, but he was driven by grander ambitions: a crusade against the Turk, and even the liberation of Constantinople. The initial stage of this project proved amazingly easy – at first. Thanks to his allies the Duke of Milan and the Medici boss of Florence, plus the temerity of the Pope, Charles advanced into Naples in early 1495 without real opposition. Contemporaries described his conquest as having been won 'with chalk' rather than with arms, a reference to his quartermasters' habit of marking the doors of houses in occupied towns with the number of

Two artillery pieces from the impressive train that accompanied Charles VIII of France in his invasion of Italy in 1494. On the left is a wrought-iron gun, while the piece on the right is cast bronze. Charles's train included eight or nine full cannon and four large culverins, as well as up to forty much smaller falcons and serpentines.

troops to be billeted. But once in possession of Naples, Charles's grand scheme evaporated. The possibility of a Valois prince adding the considerable resources of Naples to those of France stirred a diplomatic backlash, resulting in a comprehensive anti-French Holy League that included the Pope, Milan, Venice, the Habsburg emperor Maximilian and King Ferdinand of Aragon, co-ruler of Spain with his wife Isabella of Castile. In Naples, Charles was now potentially caught between the pincers of a Spanish landing and an allied invasion from the north.

To evade this disaster Charles VIII split his forces and attempted a return march to France before the League could fully muster. The sticking point came as Charles crossed the Apennines between the Ligurian coast and Parma by the valley of the Taro river; near Fornovo a mostly Venetian army waited in prepared positions. It could have been a complete French disaster, but Charles's army skilfully crossed to the opposite bank of the river, even as rising waters (there had been a storm the night before) made it difficult for the League army to follow.

The resulting battle was confused. The French suffered fewer casualties, but Venetian stradiots thoroughly sacked the French train – their booty included an erotic album with pictures of the various beauties King Charles had entertained while in Italy. Both sides claimed victory: the French for fighting their way past a trap, the League for blooding the French and sealing the collapse of Valois power in Italy. On the same day as the battle of Fornovo (6 July) the city of Naples fell to a Spanish army; further sieges and mopping up in the Neapolitan countryside lasted into early 1497.

The French were soon back in Naples. In 1500 Charles VIII's heir Louis XII signed an accord with Ferdinand of Aragon to divide the kingdom of Naples between them (it was legally the property of Ferdinand's cousin). After a successful joint invasion in 1501, the next year Ferdinand turned on his Valois partner and claimed all of the kingdom for himself. As in 1495, Ferdinand's general in Italy was Gonzalo de Cordoba, the 'Great Captain', who inflicted two sharp defeats on the French: at Cerignola in April 1503, and then at the Garigliano in December. In the first battle entrenched Spanish infantry beat off a French assault with arquebus fire. At the Garigliano Gonzalo showed his operational flair, using a flanking force to surprise and expel the French from a well-defended river line. What was left of the French Army evacuated on terms in early 1504.

This was an end to only half of Louis XII's Italian ambitions. Even before his Neapolitan adventure Louis had occupied the duchy of Milan in 1499 on an extremely slender dynastic claim. Seeking to expand from this powerful base, and putting Naples behind him, in late 1508 Louis formed the League of Cambrai with King Ferdinand, Emperor Maximilian, and the Pope. Publicly this was another Holy League aimed at the Ottoman sultan; in actuality the League's members intended to partition Venice's considerable holdings on the Italian mainland. On 14 May 1509 a French army crushed the Venetians at Agnadello in eastern Lombardy. This was Venice's worst land defeat of the Renaissance, and League armies quickly overran almost

Sixteenth-century engraving of the battle of Ravenna, 1512. This rather static print gives no sense of the battle itself, but does accurately depict contemporary military equipment and formations. The cavalry troop on the left are French men-at-arms.

every Venetian territory in the Po valley. But Venetian diplomats kept their nerve, and soon their arguments undermined the League of Cambrai. Louis XII's dramatic military success in northern Italy – like Charles VIII's a decade before in the south – quickly became a political weakness, encouraging his allies to switch before Valois power in Italy increased further. In 1511 the Pope and Ferdinand of Aragon joined with Venice to confront the King of France.

The Spanish–Papal and French armies met near Ravenna on 11 April 1512. Confident in their defensive firepower (as at Cerignola in 1503), the Spanish infantry dug in with the Ronco river to their rear: numerous cannon and war wagons studded their impressive ditch and rampart line. Despite these defences, the French Army under Gaston de Foix attacked – but not without preparation. Duke Alfonso of Ferrara, a key French ally, personally directed his own artillery to the far left wing of the French Army, from where his guns perfectly enfiladed the Spanish in their trenches. On the other flank two French guns went around to the far side of the Ronco to fire into the rear of the Spanish Army. The French suffered, too, as Spanish guns mowed lanes through

the densely formed infantry awaiting the assault. Despite this battering the French foot advanced and attacked the Spanish fortified line. Casualties on both sides were horrific. The French cavalry meanwhile chased their Spanish and Italian opposites from the field, returning to the battle to attack the Spanish infantry from behind. The Spanish foot broke; most were ridden down and killed.

OVERLEAF: THE BATTLE OF RAVENNA
The French victory at Ravenna was an impressive tactical achievement that demonstrated the increasing ability of Renaissance commanders to actually direct their armies in combat. But the victory could not prevent the further deterioration of Louis XII's position in North Italy, and bore little strategic fruit.

(1) April 1512: Gaston de Foix, nephew of King Louis XII of France and commander of the French Army in North Italy, besieges Ravenna. An allied Spanish and Papal relief army under Cardona approaches from the south

(2) 10 April 1512: Spanish master engineer Pedro Navarro directs construction of defensive earthwork line bolstered with artillery and war wagons

(3) Night of 10–11 April 1512: French engineers build pontoon bridge across the Ronco

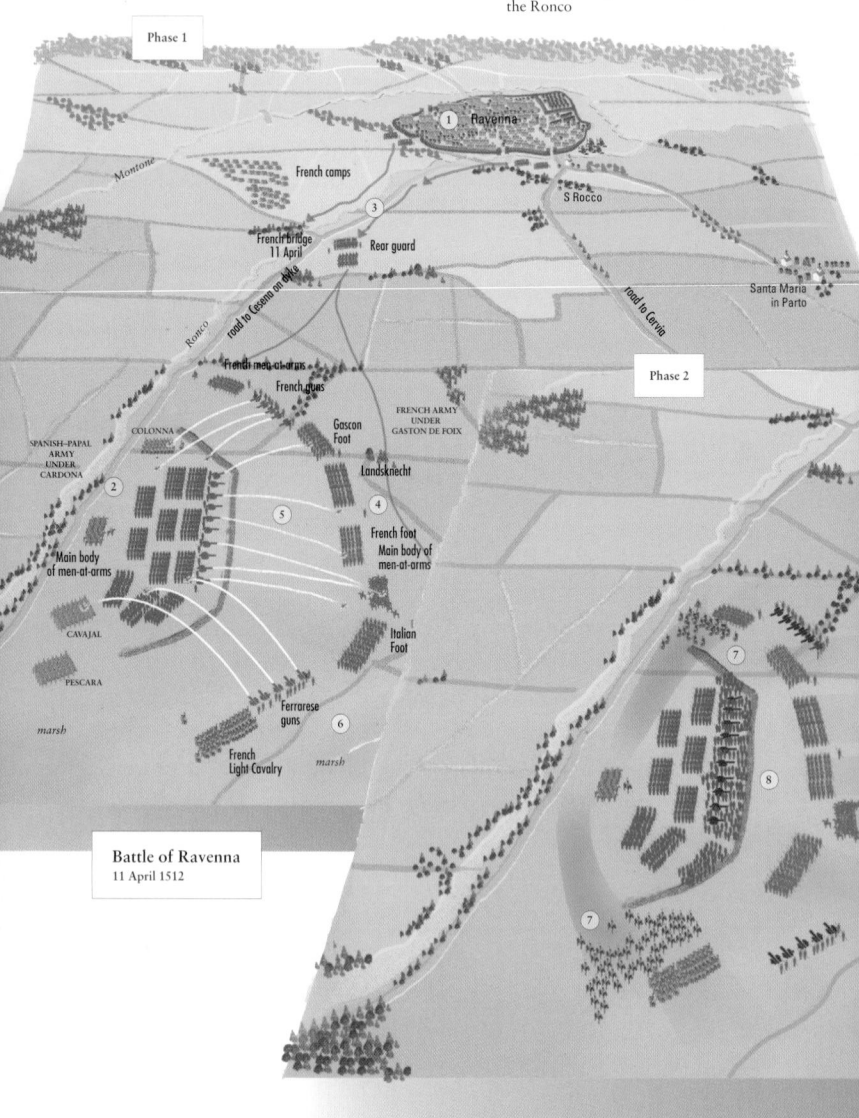

Phase 1

Montone

Ravenna

French camps

S Rocco

French bridge
11 April

Rear guard

road to Cesena on dyke

Ronco

road to Cervia

Santa Maria
in Porto

French men-at-arms

French guns

Phase 2

FRENCH ARMY
UNDER
GASTON DE FOIX

COLONNA

Gascon
Foot

SPANISH–PAPAL
ARMY
UNDER
CARDONA

Landsknecht

French foot
Main body of
men-at-arms

Main body
of men-at-arms

CAVAJAL

Italian
Foot

PESCARA

Ferrarese
guns

marsh

French
Light Cavalry

marsh

Battle of Ravenna
11 April 1512

4 Dawn of 11 April 1512: Gaston de Foix marches his army over the Ronco pontoon bridge and arranges his troops in a crescent facing the Spanish earthworks

5 Battle opens with artillery duel. Standing in open ground, the French, Gascon and landsknecht infantry take significant casualties. The Spanish infantry, lying down in their trenches, suffer less

6 The Duke of Ferrara, a key French ally, personally manoeuvres his own artillery to enfilade the Spanish foot in their trenches. Spanish losses mount

7 Mauled by artillery, the Spanish and papal men-at-arms charge their French opposites. The French win the cavalry action and begin a general chase

8 Gaston de Foix's infantry advance and engage the Spanish foot in murderous hand-to-hand combat across ditch and rampart. Casualties are extreme on both sides

9 A pair of French cannon under d'Alègre have recrossed the Ronco by pontoon bridge and pummel the Spanish army from the rear

10 The French cavalry return to the battle and strike the Spanish infantry from behind. The Spaniards finally break; only a few units maintain their discipline and make an escape. Gaston de Foix has won – but late in the day he is killed leading a charge against a stray unit of Spanish foot

Phase 3

D'Alègre's guns

9

10

Ronco

Ravenna was a great victory for Louis XII, but a fruitless one. The French Army had been mauled, and was briefly leaderless: Gaston de Foix had fallen near the end of the day. Though Spain and the Pope were neutralized, Venetian and Venetian-allied Swiss armies still pressed on Lombardy, which had to be abandoned. By the autumn of 1512, despite Ravenna, the French only held on in the citadel of Milan and other strongholds. The next year Louis sent another army over the Alps, but it was defeated by the Swiss in a dawn attack at the battle of Novara (6 June 1513). Milan was lost.

In the far north, too, 1513 was a year of trouble for Louis. Maximilian was now in the anti-French camp, and the emperor prepared to invade France in co-operation with Henry VIII of England. Henry landed at Calais in late June and took the cities of Thérouanne and Tournai over

the summer. The English also shamed a French force of men-at-arms at the battle of Guinegate (also known as the 'battle of the spurs' from the vigorous English chase), an insignificant encounter aside from the embarrassment caused to the mounted noblesse of France. Louis XII's ally James IV of Scotland invaded England, but he fell with the rest of his army at Flodden Field (9 September 1513). That same month the Swiss besieged Dijon, while the Spanish were in Navarre. Amazingly Louis managed separate truces with each of his assailants – testimony to their mutual independence and suspicion. For King Louis these settlements were his final acts of state: he died on 1 January 1515.

Louis XII's successor, Francis I, immediately took up the Valois claim to Milan, completely undaunted by his two predecessors' serial defeats. The new king crossed the Alps at the head of an army in August 1515, directly advancing against the Swiss masters of Milan. As a battle loomed Francis cleverly opened with a commercial gambit: French emissaries approached the Swiss and proposed purchasing the duchy of Milan, offering as an immediate down payment all the silver in the French camp. Perhaps half the Swiss army

Figures from a pageant procession in honour of the emperor Maximilian I. The scenes on each banner depict engagements from the emperor's 1512 campaign in Picardy against King Louis XII of France. The yellow flags with the slanted red cross of Burgundy are those of the emperor; the red flags with white crosses are those of Swiss pikemen in French pay.

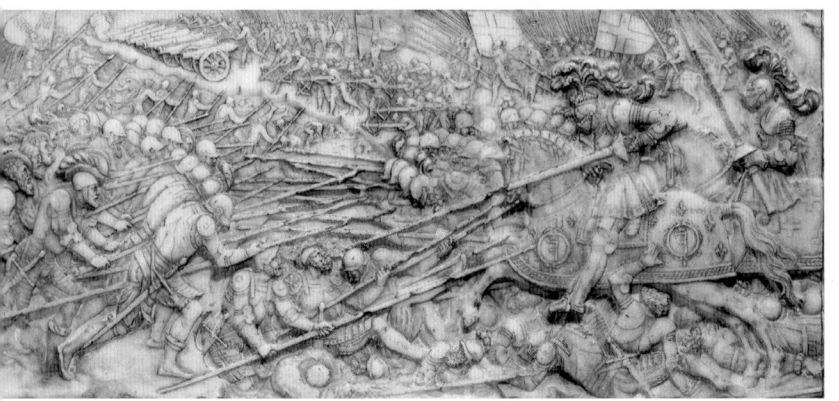

A marble relief from Francis's tomb at St Denis commemorates his great victory over the Swiss at Marignano (1515), a victory that temporarily won back the duchy of Milan.

(ruled by a committee of captains) accepted the offer and marched home. Stung by these defections the remaining Swiss angrily mustered for battle. Rather than defending the walls of Milan – the cautionary course, but not their style – the Swiss rushed out of the city to provoke a field battle at Marignano, ten miles to the south-east of Milan, on the afternoon of 13 September. Fighting lasted into the night without conclusive results. Before dawn the Swiss formed again and attacked at first light. Their bravery was unquestionable, but ferocity alone could not triumph over a larger army well supported with artillery and cavalry – the Swiss had hardly any of either. Acknowledging defeat the Swiss broke off the fight and retreated in battle order, abandoning Milan to the French. On 16 October Francis entered Milan in triumph; this was the high point of his success in Italy.

In 1519, the old emperor Maximilian I died; his successor was Charles V, already King of Spain and ruler in the Netherlands and Naples. The new emperor's ambitions, especially in Italy, were irreconcilable with those of King Francis, who had himself vainly hoped to be elected emperor. War between the two young monarchs – Charles was 19, Francis 25 – was inevitable.

The storm broke in 1521, and again Milan was the main theatre. Prospero Colonna, a gifted professional, commanded the Habsburg forces in North Italy. Without risking a major battle he took the city of Milan in a sudden escalade, and then pushed the French from most of the duchy. In the spring of 1522 Francis sent reinforcements to his general in Lombardy, the marshal Lautrec, including a large force of freshly raised Swiss. Unfortunately these pikeman had not been paid, and they insisted on attacking the Spanish Army directly – they would take booty in lieu of pay. If their request was refused, they informed Lautrec, they would abandon the French to their fate and return to Switzerland. This ultimatum forced an unwise attack on the Habsburg Army at Bicocca, between Milan and Pavia, where Colonna waited behind bastioned earthworks. If the Swiss had waited for a proper artillery preparation, as at Ravenna, the battle might have been won; instead they precipitously charged in two massive columns. Wrecked by point-blank cannon and arquebus fire, the Swiss failed to take the Imperial trenches. As at Marignano the survivors retreated in order, ending the battle: three days later the Swiss marched for home. Following Bicocca what remained of the French position in Italy disintegrated. Once again all of Lombardy was lost.

Undismayed, in 1523 Francis dispatched yet another army to Milan – an army which was promptly defeated in the following year, at the battle of the Sesia. Charles V followed this victory with an invasion of Provence from Italy. The Imperial Army besieged Marseilles in the very late summer of 1524, but was forced to evacuate. Promptly capitalizing on this Habsburg setback, Francis I personally led a large army over the Alps and into Lombardy. In late October 1524 a plague-ravaged Milan fell to Francis, and the over-confident Valois king then turned to a winter siege of Pavia. He also diverted a sizeable contingent on a mad venture against Naples – a patently stupid division of force (these troops in fact never made it south of Rome). The bulk of the Imperial Army was now in eastern Lombardy, growing in strength: it marched west to relieve Pavia in late January 1525. To prevent any rendezvous the French built an extended belt of outward-facing earthworks to the east of the city; the Spanish matched this with their own field fortifications. For three weeks the front stagnated. Then, on the night of 23 February, the Imperial relief army – wearing white shirts to ensure recognition in the darkness – marched completely around the northern wing of the French fortified line: the movement was both boldly conceived and brilliantly executed. Now marshalled in force on the French flank, the Spanish attacked at dawn the following day. Completely surprised, the French Army suffered comprehensive defeat, with King Francis himself taken captive, shattering the Valois cause in Italy. The duchy of Milan now permanently passed under the control of Charles V; it would become a vital part of the Habsburg Empire in

Europe, a rich source of men and revenue, and a crucial geographical link between Spain and Naples in the Mediterranean and Germany and the Netherlands in the north.

Following Pavia Francis was shipped to Spain, where the emperor lodged his royal captive comfortably but securely in a castle in Madrid. There Charles V firmly pressed a one-sided peace that Francis could hardly refuse. In January 1526 the Valois prisoner–king signed the

The French siege of Pavia (1525). The Imperial garrison defended the city with a belt of distinctive earthworks, many of which were captured and occupied by the French besiegers as the siege wore on. Here Swiss infantry in French service are abandoning these sconces as word spreads of the successful Imperial attack on the main French camp to the east of the city.

1. 26 October 1524: King Francis I of France occupies Milan; the Imperial garrison at Pavia, under the Spanish general de Leyva, prepares for a siege

2. 28–31 October 1524: French Army invests Pavia; the bombardment begins on 1 November

3. 2 February 1525: Imperial relief army arrives and encamps to the east of the Marmirolo hunting park

4. 3 February 1525: French begin fortification of Torre del Gallo and Five Abbeys camp to face the new Imperial threat: the besiegers are becoming the besieged

5. Night of 23–24 February: Lannoy moves his army, wearing white shirts for identification in the dark, around the eastern edge of hunting park to outflank the French and surprise them at dawn in their camp near the Castello Mirabello hunting lodge

6. Before daybreak on 24 February: Imperial engineers blast a hole in the park wall. Infantry and light cavalry pour through the breach

7. Dawn on 24 February: in conjunction with Lannoy's assault to the north, the Pavia garrison sorties and seizes the southern end of the park

8. Dawn on 24 February: Spanish arquebusiers seize Mirabello hunting lodge

9. Early morning 24 February: King Francis I, at the head of his mounted men-at-arms, charges and scatters some Imperial cavalry, but the French horse are caught standing by the advancing Imperial infantry. Surrounded and infiltrated, the French men-at-arms are individually butchered or captured. King Francis I is taken prisoner. The French Army disintegrates

10. Morning of 24 February: The French defence of the Five Abbeys collapses, and the Swiss infantry flee towards the Ticino, but the pontoon bridge is cut to prevent Imperial pursuit and thousands are killed or drowned. The French disaster is complete

THE BATTLE OF PAVIA

The Imperial commander Lannoy's night march and dawn attack on the French camp at Pavia was a bold tactical coup that completely reversed the fortunes of the campaign so far. Before the battle King Francis held Milan and was on the verge of consolidating French power in North Italy. After Pavia, Francis found himself the prisoner of his arch-rival, the emperor Charles V, and Milan was lost to the Valois forever. The wealthy and populous duchy would become the lynchpin of the Habsburg Empire in Europe.

Battle of Pavia
1525

The night march at Pavia (1525). To break the deadlock of the siege lines, over the night of 23–24 February the Imperial relief army made a daring march through darkness to outflank the French besiegers. At the bottom of this painting Imperial arquebusiers wear white shirts for better identification in the gloom.

Treaty of Madrid, formally yielding all his claims in Italy – and much else besides. The agreement freed Francis to return to his kingdom in March, but he had no intention of keeping his pledge. Instead he immediately prepared for a renewed war, and in May he formed the anti-Habsburg League of Cognac with Venice and Pope Clement VII. Their goal was to undo the work of Pavia, but the League's military operations were entirely lacklustre and ineffective.

The emperor's soldiers performed almost too well. In 1527 a rather ragtag Habsburg Army under the constable Bourbon – a renegade subject of King Francis – moved to confront the Pope. On 6 May this unlikely force succeeded in breaking into Rome, with Bourbon slain by a stray ball just as his troops entered the city. Pope Clement hurriedly fled across town to his Castello St Angelo fortress, while uncontrollable Habsburg soldiers began a thorough and extended sack of the city. The riotous soldiery profaned as well as tortured, raped and ransomed. Some of these men, German Protestant landsknechts, scratched the slogan 'long live Pope Luther' on Vatican frescoes. Others used crucifixes for target practice. Stories spread of common whores dressing in costly, sacred priestly robes, and drunken soldiers feeding the communion host to animals. Bottled up in his castle, the Pope was almost as much Charles V's prisoner as King Francis after Pavia, but the Imperial soldiers' merciless sack of the Holy City was also a humiliation for Charles, and a public relations disaster – news of the brutal proceedings

The Pope's Castel Sant'Angelo fortress in Rome was built on top of the immense drum of the ancient emperor Hadrian's ruined family mausoleum. The medieval fortress was modernized by the infamous Borgia Pope Alexander VI at the turn of the sixteenth century, a project which included the addition of bastions for artillery. The popes were among the earliest, most progressive patrons of Renaissance military architecture.

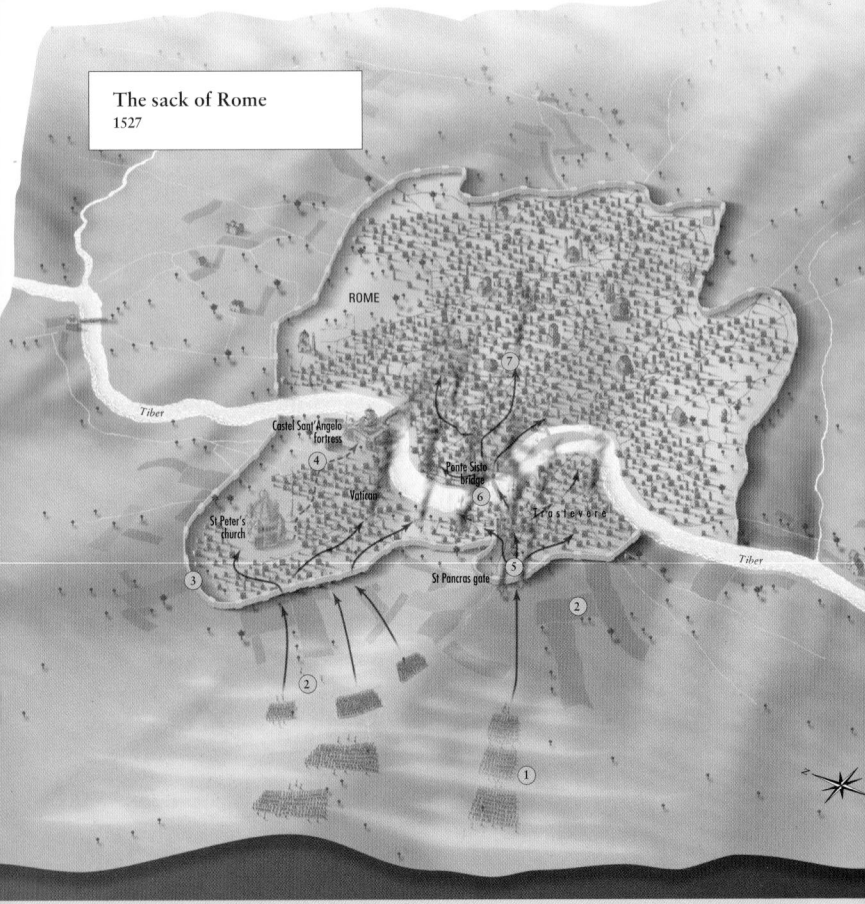

The sack of Rome
1527

ROME

Tiber

Castel Sant'Angelo
fortress

4

Ponte Sisto
bridge

7

6

Vatican

St Peter's
church

Trastevere

3

St Pancras gate

Tiber

5

2

2

1

① Afternoon of 5 May 1527: an ill-fed and ill-disciplined Imperial Army under the renegade French constable Bourbon reaches Rome. Facing the disintegration of his army, Bourbon decides on an immediate attack

② 6 May: before dawn the Imperial Army advances to assault the Vatican and Trastevere walls. Early in the attack Bourbon is struck and killed by an arquebus

③ Covered by a heavy early-morning fog, some Spanish soldiers discover and open up a badly-barricaded cellar window in the outer walls. Others enter through a low-level gunport

④ By mid morning the defending papal commanders are aware that some Imperial soldiers are inside the walls. Pope Clement VII and other prelates flee from the Vatican palace to the Castel Sant'Angelo. Other refugees cram and block the bridges across the Tiber

⑤ The St Pancras gate is battered down and substantial numbers of Imperial soldiers enter Trastevere

⑥ Late afternoon 6 May: against negligible opposition, Imperial infantry seize the Ponte Sisto bridge across the Tiber

⑦ Leaderless after the death of Bourbon, the battle-mad Imperial soldiers – both Spanish Catholics and German Lutherans – pillage the churches, palaces and storehouses of the city for weeks on end. Clement VII watches the destruction of the Holy City from the safety of Castel Sant'Angelo. The Pope is cornered, but the behaviour of the Imperial soldiery is a humiliation for Emperor Charles V

THE SACK OF ROME

Even in a century full of military horrors the sack of Rome stood out. With their commander killed and the city in their hands, the Imperial soldiery ran amok. They raped, tortured and burned, pausing only to thoroughly plunder the city's many rich churches and palaces.

raced through Europe. In a decade of electrifying news, the sack of Rome was perhaps the most stunning and most disturbing to the average European. Would Luther indeed become Pope? Or would the Turk be the next to despoil Rome?

Clement and Charles made a deal. The Pope would now support the emperor, and in return Charles would assist in the Medici Pope's recovery of Florence (the city had revolted with news of the fall of Rome). Ideally the partners would then confront the sultan Süleyman. A successful Imperial siege of Florence took place in 1530, a few months after Clement crowned Charles emperor in the papal city of Bologna – though he had been elected in 1519, politics had prevented a formal coronation. (Given the events of 1527, a ceremony in Rome itself was out of the question.) In the meantime, an amazing French attempt to take Naples in the summer of 1528 had utterly failed after the Genoese admiral Andrea Doria switched sides from Valois to Habsburg, ending the French expedition's hope of support by sea. At the moment of his coronation in 1530, Charles V was unquestionably the most powerful prince in Christendom.

Back in France King Francis fumed and schemed – and challenged Charles to personal combat, an indication of his frustration. Across the Channel, Francis's anti-Habsburg partner King Henry VIII genially seconded the challenge. More usefully Francis searched for new allies, reaching out to the Protestant princes of Germany and even to the sultan Süleyman, who had already smashed Hungary (1526) and battered at the gates of Vienna (1529). All things considered, the Ottomans would prove to be the best Valois ally of the next generation; events had certainly moved the Valois King of France a long, long way from 1494, when Charles VIII had dreamed of a grand crusade against Constantinople.

His preparations complete, in 1536 Francis I returned to war in Italy, but less rashly than in the past. His armies successfully occupied Savoy and Piedmont, potential bases for the recovery of Milan: this was the most substantial French military achievement in Italy since Marignano. Charles V replied with his second invasion of Provence, which petered out as had the first (in 1524). In the summer of 1538 both sides agreed to a ten-year truce.

It did not last. The war resumed in 1543, with both sides now co-operating closely with allies. Along the Riviera the French linked up with the sultan's fleet under Barbarossa: together they sacked the town of Nice, and Toulon was evacuated of its Christian citizens to make an Ottoman naval base, complete with mosque, over the winter of 1543–4. In Piedmont a Spanish army was defeated at the battle of Ceresole (1544), which confirmed the French position in north-western Italy, but there was no following attempt on Milan.

The northern campaigns of 1544 proved as cautious and indecisive. Henry VIII had broken with his Valois ally in 1543, and the next year he landed the largest English army of the Renaissance – over 30,000 men – in northern France. Henry's goal was nothing less than the seizure of Paris, operating in tandem with an Imperial force invading through Champagne under Charles V's personal command. It was a potentially very powerful strategy, but both Imperial and English offensive operations bogged, the emperor's in front of St Dizier, which fell after a month's siege, and Henry's before the city of Boulogne, which fell on 14 September 1544. On 9 October the French attempted to win the city back by a camisade, a sudden night assault with the men wearing white shirts (camises), such as the Spanish had performed so brilliantly at Pavia. The assault was initially successful, but the French attackers prematurely turned to plundering the city and were routed by an English counter-attack. King Henry thus kept his small conquest, though the opportunity of snatching Paris had been lost. Charles V having already made a separate peace with the French king in September of 1544 (just days before the fall of Boulogne), Henry VIII settled as well.

King Francis I died in 1547. His son Henry II waited for five years before renewing the Valois challenge to the Habsburg emperor. Then, after allying with the Protestant princes of Germany in late 1551, between April and July of the following year Henry quickly seized the three Imperial cities of Metz, Toul and Verdun. Charles V's response, a gruelling late-season siege of Metz, failed – what was left of the Habsburg Army after ten weeks in open trenches evacuated on 26 December 1552. The continuing war followed a pattern of enormous efforts, particularly in siege operations, with few accomplishments beyond individual places taken. In the summer of 1553 the French retook Thérouanne from England. The next year a cavalry action at Renty proved a meaningless French success. Henry also intervened in Italy, sending a French expedition to succour the Siennese in their revolt from Medici and Spanish domination. The French commander Montluc ably directed the defence of Siena, but the city fell in 1555.

In the same year Charles V began an orderly abdication, giving Spain (together with its overseas empire), Milan, Naples and the Netherlands to his son Philip. The Habsburg homeland in Austria was kept by Charles's brother Ferdinand, who became emperor in 1558. Under Philip II of Spain the Habsburg–Valois war continued almost by inertia. A final French attempt on Naples in 1557 was no more successful than any previous expedition of the past sixty-odd years. In the north a French army sought to relieve the Habsburg siege of St Quentin, but instead it was destroyed in battle (10 August 1557). A signal French success followed: the seizure of Calais from the English (6 January 1558).

There was time for one more great defeat in Henry II's reign. In the summer of 1558 a small French army entered Habsburg Flanders with no strategic intent other than plunder. It lingered too long before turning back for the safe base of Calais. Burdened with loot and so

Campaigns in Northern France
1552–8

→ Valois movements

→ Habsburg movements

— border 1547

--- border 1559

CAMPAIGNS IN NORTHERN FRANCE, 1552–8

In the 1550s the most significant actions of the Habsburg–Valois wars took place on the northern front, along the border between France and the Holy Roman Empire.

(1) April–October 1552: Henry II seizes Metz, Verdun, Nancy and reaches Strasbourg

(2) 19 October 1552 – 1 January 1553: Imperial siege fails to retake Metz for Charles V

(3) 10 August 1557: French Army routed in failure to relieve Imperial siege of St Quentin

(4) September 1557: despite victory at St Quentin, the Imperial Army disperses at Cambrai – there is neither the cash at hand nor time left in the campaign year for an invasion of France

(5) 7 January 1558: French seize Calais from England

(6) 13 July 1558: Raiding French Army caught and destroyed at Gravelines

(7) 2 April 1559: peace at Câteau Cambrésis ends sixty-five years of dynastic war between Habsburg and Valois. France keeps Metz and Verdun, but recognizes Habsburg possession of Naples and Milan and Spanish dominance in the Mediterranean

(8) 30 June 1559: Henry II mortally wounded at tournament celebrating peace

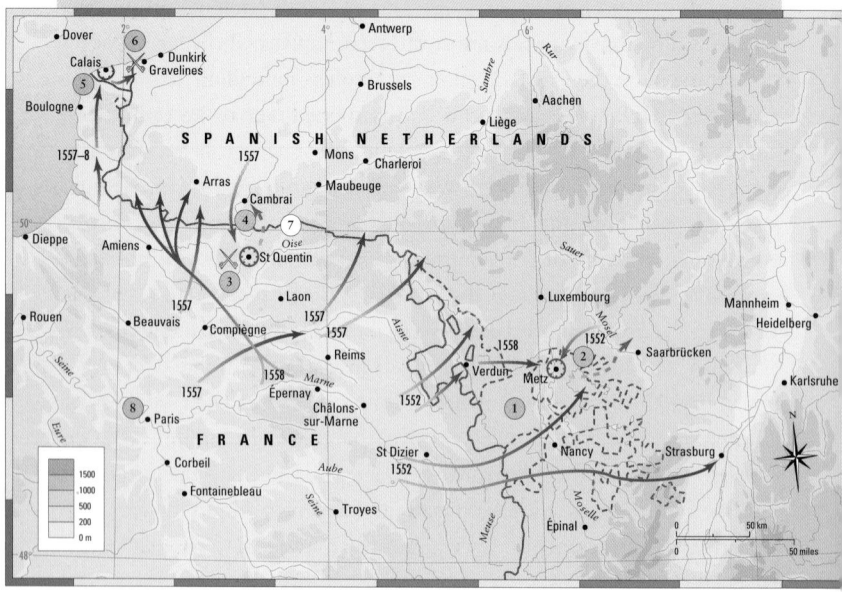

already half undone with ill discipline, the French raiders were caught by a larger Habsburg army and forced to make a stand near Gravelines on 13 July 1558. Their backs were to the sea, where a Habsburg-allied English naval squadron proceeded to bombard the French formations. The ensuing battle was lopsided and the French army was destroyed. Gravelines put an end to Henry II's interest in sustaining the war. He was old and unwell, and his opponents were willing to treat. All parties desired peace, and real peace – not an armistice in which to prepare for renewed campaigns.

Terms were reached at Câteau Cambrésis in 1559. Henry would keep Metz, Toul and Verdun – of little concern to Philip II of Spain, anyway – but evacuate Savoy and Piedmont in Italy (excepting some garrisons). This was a particular vindication for the exiled duke of Savoy, who had commanded the victorious Habsburg Army at St Quentin in 1557. From the perspective of France, though the treaty was welcome, its conditions were scanty. Four succeeding generations of Valois kings had copiously poured the treasure and blood of their kingdom into Italy – and all for naught. Against the French, the Habsburgs had won by keeping what their rivals could not: Naples and Milan.

So often unlucky in war, the Valois turned out to be even more unlucky in peace. In a freak accident just four months after the agreement at Câteau Cambrésis, the captain of Henry II's own Scottish guards mortally wounded the king during a jousting tournament put on in Paris as part of the festivities celebrating the new peace. In the spirit of this peace Philip II dispatched his own physician, the great Vesalius, from Brussels to Paris, but to no avail. Henry II's unexpected death in the summer of 1559 put a capstone on the venomous Habsburg–Valois rivalry that had dominated the internal politics of Renaissance Europe since the turn of the century. Conflict between France and Spain would return in the second half of the sixteenth century, but not substantially in Italy, and this new round of wars was bound up and connected by an even greater and deeper European feud: that between Catholics and Protestants.

CHAPTER SIX

Faith versus Faith

A military procession of the Paris militia of the Holy or Catholic League, c. 1588. During the last stages of the French Religious Wars Paris was the centre of Catholic resistance to the possibility that the Huguenot leader, Henry of Navarre, might ascend the throne of France. The idea of a Calvinist king outraged many of the Catholic faithful. Here a militant column of Franciscans, Dominicans and other clerics marches through the centre of Paris. The red cross of Lorraine on some hats was the symbol of the Guise family, leaders of the League. By 1588 France had suffered thirty years of intermittent, brutal civil war.

Faith versus Faith

A**T THE HUMAN LEVEL** the Reformation was a crisis of conscience, as individual believing Christians struggled to identify the true faith in their hearts and minds, balancing custom with scripture, and reason with prayer. For a few remarkable generations the arguments for and against religious change – either within or without the existing Catholic church – dominated the spiritual life of Europe. This great watershed event in the larger history of Christianity is conventionally

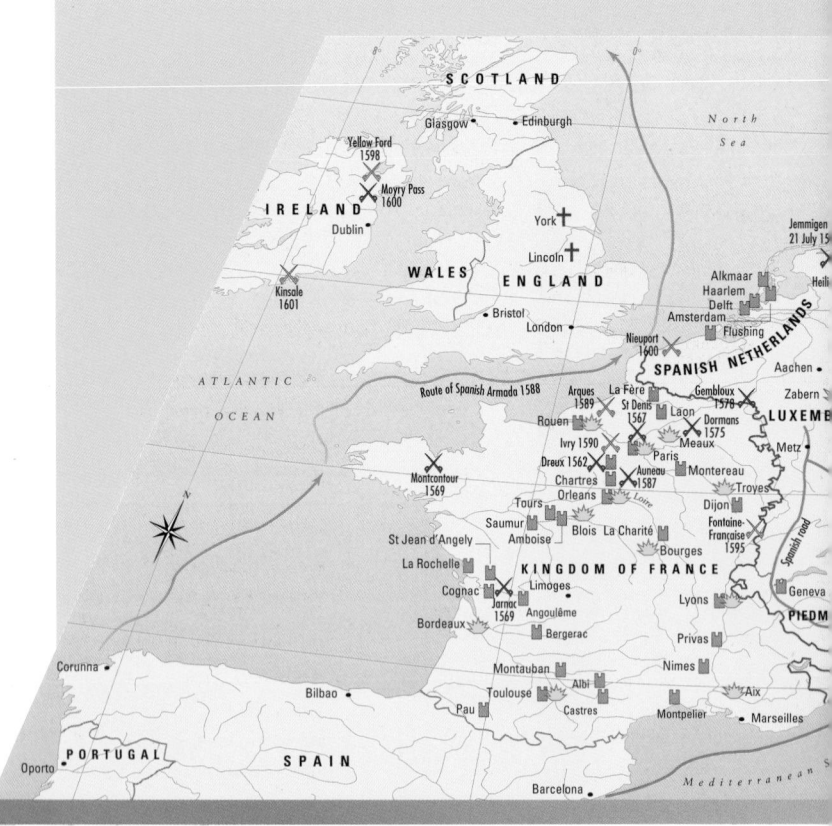

dated from 1517, when the renegade Augustinian friar Martin Luther nailed his famous ninety-five theses to the church door at Wittenberg in Germany, publicly challenging all comers to a debate on the eternal and fundamental principles of Christ's church on earth. But the great questions had anticipated Luther. Throughout Renaissance Europe concerned Christians were already wrestling with the myriad problems of the late medieval church, which almost everyone agreed was deeply compromised by abuse and corruption, from an unseemly love of politics and luxury among the aptly named princes of the church (the

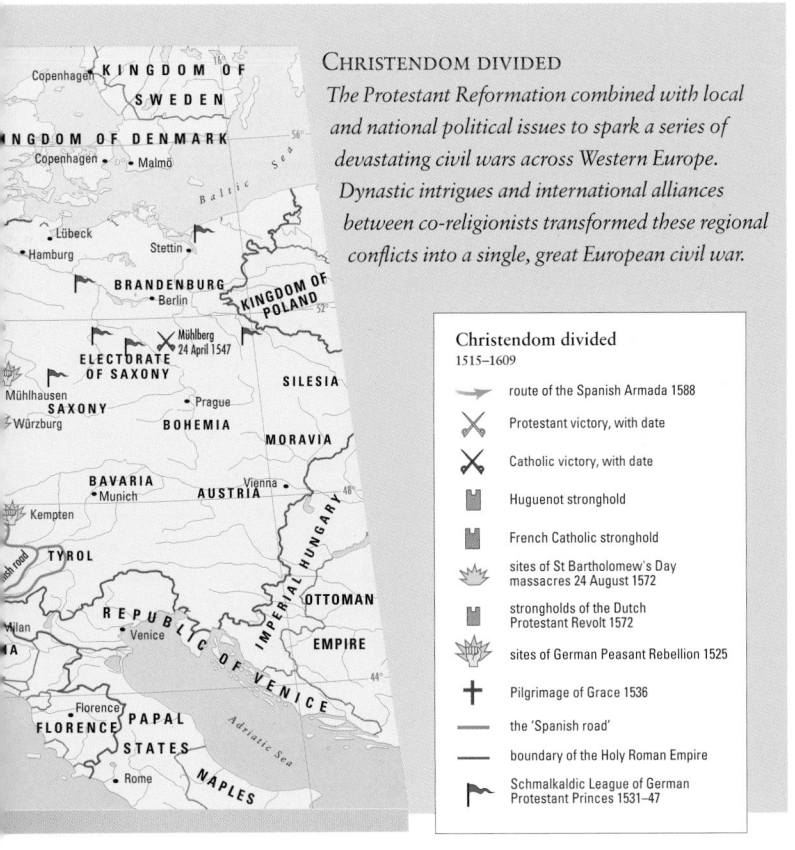

CHRISTENDOM DIVIDED

The Protestant Reformation combined with local and national political issues to spark a series of devastating civil wars across Western Europe. Dynastic intrigues and international alliances between co-religionists transformed these regional conflicts into a single, great European civil war.

Christendom divided
1515–1609

↗ route of the Spanish Armada 1588

✕ Protestant victory, with date

✕ Catholic victory, with date

▯ Huguenot stronghold

▯ French Catholic stronghold

✾ sites of St Bartholomew's Day massacres 24 August 1572

▯ strongholds of the Dutch Protestant Revolt 1572

✾ sites of German Peasant Rebellion 1525

✝ Pilgrimage of Grace 1536

—— the 'Spanish road'

—— boundary of the Holy Roman Empire

⚑ Schmalkaldic League of German Protestant Princes 1531–47

powerful bishops, cardinals and popes), to an unfortunate moral laxity and doctrinal ignorance among the lower clergy and general laity. The very pervasiveness of contemporary concern helps explain the social and political explosion that followed Luther's challenge to Rome.

Confrontational church reform movements, even religious wars within Christendom, were nothing new in 1517. Across the Middle Ages religious rebels (who were often rebels against the state as well) had several times seriously challenged the theology and authority of Rome, most recently with the Hussite revolt in Bohemia in the early fifteenth century. The Hussites had even won some measure of spiritual self-determination. A century later, in Luther's time, the faults and issues which had ignited Bohemia in the days of Jan Hus were still alive and still unresolved. A coming crisis was certain. The real question was whether that crisis – the Reformation – would amount to a reform of the Roman church, or its replacement: could over a thousand years of tradition still be used to guide the faithful, or must every scrap of doctrine, and every layer of hierarchy and bureaucracy, be purged and formed anew?

On the one hand, men like Erasmus of Rotterdam, a contemporary of Luther and a scathing critic of papal arrogance, refused to break with Rome. There were others of the same stamp. An internal Catholic reform movement coalesced and gained power from the 1540s, leading the church through the Council of Trent (1545–63) and a consequent reformulation of authority, belief and practice, and inspiring a moral regeneration among the clergy and lay faithful. On the other hand, Martin Luther concluded, by at least 1521 – the year of his famous confrontation with Charles V at the imperial Diet in Worms – that the church must be recreated on an apostolic model, and the existing Roman church dismantled or destroyed. Other dissenting theologians agreed, but of course on their own terms. Zwingli in Zurich, Calvin in Geneva and Bucer in Strasburg all echoed Luther's call for a church reborn, but their specific prescriptions differed. Every issue was potentially the stuff of further schism: what was the true nature of the eucharist, a remembrance or a miracle? Were images a legitimate aid to faith, or scandalous idols? An ongoing sixteenth-century Reformation did not neatly split Europe into two camps, Catholic and Protestant, but at least half a dozen: besides different shades of Catholic, Lutheran and Calvinist, the Anabaptists, Socinians and other minor groups entangled the theology and politics of reform to no end. It is only a convenience to speak of Protestant and Catholic as if either group – even Catholic – were a monolith.

If the Reformation was a personal crisis for the individual Christian, it was also a civil war for Christian Europe. It could hardly have been otherwise, since those Christians debating their own faith included the crowned heads of Europe – and also their independent-minded subjects, great and small. Within and between state borders religious difference naturally led to political confrontation, and reconciliation proved elusive and difficult. Very few imagined that the political complications of reform could be obviated by the modern formulae of widespread toleration and individual freedom of conscience; rather, the committed on all sides believed that only one possible interpretation of Christianity could be lawful – all others were heresy. Thus friction and war were inevitable.

Inside states the religious conflict often took the form of judicial action. In Spain the magistrates of the Inquisition investigated their cases, wrote up massive documents detailing the persons and issues at hand, and then, if a recantation of serious unorthodoxy did not take place, the refusers were handed over to civil authorities for punishment, sometimes en masse and in public at an auto-da-fé, or 'demonstration of faith'. It was thus that the small Protestant communities in Seville and Valladolid – and in Naples in Spanish Italy – were winkled out and eradicated. In Venice the Catholic authorities, characteristically enough, chose a more devious course: known Protestants (who might refuse to attend mass or close their shops during religious processions) were seized from their homes in the dead of night and then drowned in the lagoon. These semi-secret disappearances made the point as well as a public execution: Venice might have her arguments with the Pope, but only orthodox Catholicism would be tolerated among the Christian population of the city. Protestant Europe was by no means above persecution. Calvin's Geneva did not hesitate to use the bonfire to enforce its particular brand of reform, most notoriously burning the radical anti-trinitarian Michael Servetus.

The European religious struggle gradually gained a more formal military identity, particularly as individual princes, motivated both by conscience and by opportunity, embraced different strains and strengths of Protestantism. In general the initial political success of the Protestant cause was directly related to physical distance from Rome. Without exception, the rulers of Iberia and Italy remained Catholic, while in far northern Europe Roman supremacy disappeared almost without a ripple: in Sweden the king easily enforced a state Lutheranism, while the last Grand Master of the Teutonic Knights gave up his vows, took a wife and made himself Duke of Prussia. The real contested space between Protestant and Catholic lay in the middle ground between north and south, from west to east across Ireland, England, France, the Netherlands, Switzerland, the Holy Roman Empire, Bohemia, Hungary and Poland. In all of these areas the division between new and old religious loyalties fragmented existing polities, and often exacerbated existing social and political tensions. It is not surprising that the ensuing wars were often particularly vicious affairs.

The religious wars of the sixteenth century can be divided chronologically into two periods. First, from the 1520s through the middle of the century, the religious conflicts tended to be smaller in scale, localized, and less well connected to wars elsewhere in Europe. Salient examples include the Peasants' Revolt in the Holy Roman Empire (1524–6), the destruction of Anabaptist Münster (1535), the Pilgrimage of Grace in England (1536) and the Schmalkaldic War in Germany (1546–7). This period was followed, in the second half of the century, by a second round of larger and longer religious wars. These conflicts were still obviously civil in nature – the two greatest struggles were those in France and the Netherlands – but they were also tightly connected across state boundaries by policy and strategy, as well as by confessional affection. Particular convergence took place in north-western Europe in the 1580s and 1590s, as King Philip II of Spain simultaneously attempted to defeat an entrenched rebellion in the Netherlands, invade England and ensure the victory of Catholic over Huguenot in France.

The first great conflict of the Reformation era was the German Peasants' Revolt of 1524–6. The war was actually not one seamless event, but a series of essentially uncoordinated regional revolts. The uprisings began in the Black Forest, and then spread north to Württemberg, Franconia and Saxony, and south and east to the Tyrol. Unrest was widespread but uneven; it travelled like wildfire, touching some districts and skipping over others. The rebellion remained a phenomenon of the countryside: most larger towns were aloof, and were usually immune behind their walls. This lack of urban support was a critical rebel weakness. In most areas the trouble began with open meetings and demonstration marches by disaffected tenants and oppressed serfs. Talk then turned to direct action against local oppressors: landlords were burned out, and there were atrocities, most dramatically a massacre of feudal lords at Weinsberg in April 1525. Local victories gave the rebels confidence, and their bands grew to become small armies; many columns marched under the

The German artist Albrecht Dürer sympathized with the rebellious German peasants and designed a monument to their plight and destruction. The memorial was never built, but Dürer did publish his design: an exhausted, despairing peasant – a sword plunged through his shoulders – sits atop a column symbolizing the fruits of his labour.

banner of the peasant's shoe, a symbol borrowed from earlier risings. Thus some common tradition of rural revolt connected the separate peasant bands, but central political direction remained minimal and many opportunities for co-operation were missed. Some peasant armies, particularly that of the Lake Constance region, were militarily formidable; others were rabble. By the spring of 1525, however, the political integrity of the empire was seriously at stake.

The authorities responsible for suppressing the rebellious peasantry were the Swabian League of imperial nobles and, more distantly, Emperor Charles V, who, over the autumn and early winter of 1524–5, had to divide his attention and resources between the situation in Germany and Francis I's dangerous invasion of North Italy. To face the peasants, command of Imperial and Habsburg troops was given to George von Waldburg, an experienced captain who prudently acted with audacity or caution as the situation demanded. His opponents were not necessarily negligible soldiers; many of the peasants were veterans of landsknecht companies, while almost all had some militia experience. However, many rebel bands were ill-equipped with firearms, and naturally enough the peasants were desperately short of mounted men – cavalry of course being the military expression of the nobility. Von Waldburg easily routed the smaller and less well-armed bands, and he successfully negotiated with the more dangerous. Interestingly, many of the German troops that came north over the Alps after the emperor's great victory at Pavia in early 1525 refused to take part in the campaign: they would have nothing to do with the slaughter of their poor countrymen. Other professional companies refused as well. The decisive battle of this awkward, unpleasant civil war came at Königshofen on the Tauber river (2 June 1525). There, together with an action at Ingolstadt a few days later, a large Franconian peasant army was twice defeated, ridden down by the horsemen of the Swabian League. These disasters sealed the rebels' overall defeat.

The Peasants' Revolt closely followed or coincided with the first great motions of the Protestant Reformation, but the rebels and their humble leaders were by no means the creatures of Luther or Zwingli. In many cases the peasants were more extreme in their ideas and goals than the magisterial Protestant theologians. A savage anticlericalism frequently inflamed the peasants' grievances and actions, and their war aims at times approached a social and political revolution. In certain villages local Reformations, which often included the enthusiastic destruction of images (roadside shrines and crucifixes as well as church paintings and sculptures), seem to have inspired or prepared for further violent action against feudal authorities. There was also some sense of a greater project afoot: the peasant bands of the Black Forest swore themselves to a Christian Union with an elaborate constitution, as did those of Upper Swabia. Church reform was only one plank of these compacts. Surviving documents testify to the peasants' desire for a divine social justice, and the foundation of a new political order defined by the 'word of God' and the revelations of the gospels. Among the peasants' leaders was the radical theologian Thomas Müntzer, who preached an apocalyptic holy war that would topple the powerful and replace them with the righteous and humble. His followers fought beneath the banner of the rainbow, God's own sign, which did not prevent their defeat and massacre at the battle of Frankenhausen (15 May 1525). The peasants received little support from the established Protestant leaders. As the events of the risings unfolded, Luther himself moved from general sympathy to outright hostility, penning a tract – 'Against the Robbing and Thieving Hordes of Peasants' – that encouraged the rebellion's murderous suppression.

The end of the Peasants' Revolt was not an end to the radical Reformation. In Münster, an ecclesiastical city in northern Germany, a faction of Anabaptists took over the town government in 1533, and in the following year they proclaimed a new 'Kingdom of Zion'. Biblical extremists, the Münster Anabaptists practised not only adult baptism – a scandal to both Catholics and moderate Protestants – but polygamy on the model of the Old Testament. They were also early communists, dividing property among all true believers. Those who did not accept adult rebaptism were expelled, and dissenters within this dissenting community were violently reproved. The Catholic prince–bishop of Münster raised an army which retook the city in 1535 after a protracted and horrific siege of sixteen months: the last desperate defenders of the Anabaptist kingdom fell defending a wagon laager in the central market place. The surviving leaders were publicly tortured to death. Münster was only an incident, though an exceedingly bloody and sensational one, but like the Peasants' Revolt it highlighted a key political consequence of the Reformation message – the ease with which calls for religious reform could combine with other grievances to spark a political and social explosion.

Revolt and suppression also took place in Protestant lands. The year after the fall of Münster a Catholic rebellion of similar scale – although with a reactionary rather than a revolutionary agenda – convulsed

The fall of Anabaptist Münster, 1535. The siege of Münster was a tiny religious war between the radical religious zealots of the 'Kingdom of Zion' and a besieging army of the Catholic prince–bishop, expelled in 1533. The rebels held out for over a year before their defences collapsed. Note the earthwork fortifications surrounding the city, including circular sconces.

Lincolnshire and Yorkshire in northern England: the Pilgrimage of Grace. This was the only immediate military opposition to Henry VIII's limited Reformation. The pilgrimage was led by local notables and ecclesiastics, including the archbishop of York. They demanded a return to papal fealty, and an end to the dissolution of the monasteries – Henry's financial windfall from the break with Rome. Economic concerns, particularly against the enclosure of common lands, motivated some commoner followers. (As in south Germany in the previous decade, one source of unrest was the innovations and inequities of a quickening European economy.) In England in 1536 there was no major battle between king and rebels. Instead the revolt was defused by negotiation, which Henry's lieutenants followed up with judicial action against the ringleaders. A few hundred were executed. Then in 1549 a second great Catholic rising against Protestant rule, Kett's Rebellion, took place in southern England. The rebels were easily smashed at the battle of Dussindale (27 August 1549).

Back in Germany, Emperor Charles V faced a strong and politically well-founded Protestant opposition to his authority: the Schmalkaldic League, formed in 1531 by the leading Lutheran princes of the Holy Roman Empire. For fifteen years after the founding of the League, repeated attempts at negotiating a religious peace in the empire all failed, but interim agreements did hold at bay a major armed conflict between Charles and his Protestant subjects – who insisted that they remained loyal, despite the military and financial arrangements made at Schmalkalden. From the emperor's point of view these agreements were temporary and unsatisfactory solutions; Valois interventions in Italy, and above all the overwhelming threat of the Ottoman sultan to the east, essentially forced him to keep the peace in the empire. The Treaty of Crépy in 1544 between Charles V and King Francis I of France finally gave the emperor his opportunity to plan a confrontation with the Protestant princes of Germany. (King Francis similarly seized the moment to repress his own religious minority, in Provence in the spring of 1545.)

Open war between Charles V and the Schmalkaldic League began in 1546, delayed until Charles could negotiate a truce with the sultan Süleyman. Charles was also diplomatically active within the empire, secretly detaching a middling prince, Duke Maurice of Saxony, from the Schmalkaldic League, and even making him a closet Imperial ally. Maurice was a cousin – an ambitious and unscrupulous cousin – to the more important prince the elector John Frederick of Saxony. This defection and alliance remained unknown to the other League members. Hostilities opened in the summer of 1546, with League operations in southern Germany catching the emperor off guard. By the autumn a substantial Habsburg force had gathered, and faced the League army at Ingolstadt in Bavaria. With the League concentrated against the emperor in the south, to the north Maurice of Saxony suddenly invaded the lands of his cousin the Saxon elector. The

A landsknecht company council, a detail of the camp of the Schmalkaldic League army at the siege of Wolfenbuttel, 1542. The mercenary landsknecht companies were democracies of a sort, with community discussions of community concerns. The forum for such conversations was a special ring formation where grumblings could be distilled into concrete demands. Note the landsknechts' straw huts, built around their pikes.

surprise move transformed the war, as the elector John Frederick marched north with much of the Schmalkaldic League army to recover his lands in Saxony. The Imperial Army under Charles V's personal command now aggressively switched to the offensive and also marched north, rendezvousing first with a force under the emperor's brother, the archduke Ferdinand of Austria, and then with Maurice.

Charles's enlarged army met up with the League at Mühlberg on the Elbe, with the river separating the two forces. On the very early morning of 24 April 1547 a body of Spanish infantry crossed the Elbe by a ford that was unknown and unguarded by the Saxons. A speedily improvised pontoon bridge then allowed the crossing of more Habsburg soldiers, as well as a few artillery pieces. Panicking in the face of this sudden advance in force, the League commanders first ordered a general evacuation of their camp, but then attempted to form for combat when pursuing Imperial cavalry caught the fleeing columns in mid retreat. Badly led and thoroughly rattled, the League army disintegrated over the course of a full day of battle: Mühlberg was a comprehensive Protestant defeat, and it all but ended the larger war. Among other Lutheran leaders the elector John Frederick was captured; his lands and electoral dignity were eventually transferred to the enterprising Maurice of Saxony.

Mühlberg seemed a second Pavia, but Charles V found little profit in his crushing of the Schmalkaldic League. Despite the emperor's overwhelming military victory, the Protestant cause in the empire refused to shrivel. To have enforced a complete religious settlement to his liking Charles would have had to besiege and take every Protestant stronghold in Germany, one by one. It was a task he did not have the material strength to undertake, nor the political opportunity. In 1555 (after a further spasm of war in 1551–2) the exhausted and ailing emperor agreed to the religious peace of Augsburg, which granted the princes of the empire the right to determine the ruling faith in their own territories, as long as that choice was between Catholicism and Lutheranism – other creeds were proscribed. For the emperor Augsburg was a galling compromise, a tacit political defeat. He would soon relinquish imperial affairs to his brother Ferdinand. Charles's continuing frustrations in Germany even after Mühlberg clearly demonstrated the limitations of military force in undoing the work of Reformation. Future religious wars would further underline those limitations.

The next round of religious wars opened in France, where the unexpected death of Henry II in 1559 ushered in thirty-five years of royal weakness and internal strife. Henry's immediate successor, the teenaged Francis II, reigned for barely a year; he was succeeded by Henry's second son, the 10-year-old Charles IX. Henry's widowed queen, the shrewd and capable Florentine princess Catherine de' Medici, picked up the pieces and served as regent. She would continue to be a force at court long after Charles, an uninspiring and mentally suspect man, reached his majority. Catherine eventually rallied the royal cause

The siege of Frankfurt am Main by Maurice of Saxony, 1552. During the Schmalkaldic War (1546–7) Maurice had been Charles V's secret ally in the Protestant camp. In 1552 Maurice turned against the emperor to league with King Henry II of France. While Henry took Metz and Verdun, Maurice attempted to take Frankfurt, but the Imperial defence proved too strong. French intervention in Germany significantly complicated the emperor's attempts to force a Catholic settlement on the empire.

in the name of her sons – three would rule France – but in the meantime a few crucial years had been lost to dynastic flux and confusion. France descended towards a complicated, many-sided civil war.

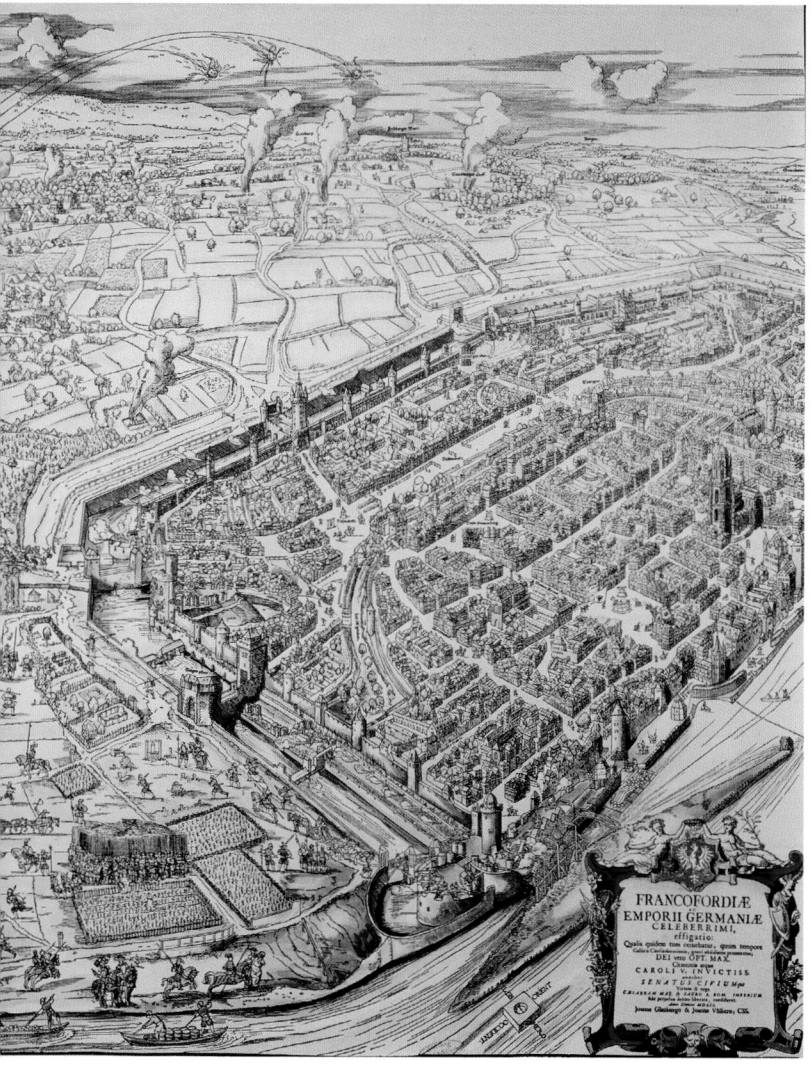

The French crisis was in part purely political, as the most prominent and ambitious noble families of the realm jockeyed both with each other, and with the crown, for position and power. This competition would only intensify as it became clear that Catherine's three sons, the last Valois kings of France, would remain without legitimate issue. The struggle in France was also, of course, about religion. Calvinism had found many converts, particularly in the south and west, and also within some of the greatest noble houses. Faith and family therefore determined the factions. The most powerful Catholic party was that of the Guise; their rival–allies included the Montmorency. Several clans shared – and squabbled over – leadership of the French Protestants, or Huguenots. Among these men were Gaspard de Coligny and the Bourbon princes of Condé. The Valois remained staunchly Catholic, but Catherine de' Medici was profoundly – and correctly – suspicious of the Guise. She also rightly concluded that her own family had the most to lose by civil war, and so Catherine was often, but not always, one of the foremost promoters of settlement and peace. In January of 1562 she promoted a royal edict that granted Huguenots the right to worship openly.

Toleration proved no solution to the French crisis, as a particularly provocative act of violence forced a civil war. On 1 March 1562 the armed entourage of the Duke of Guise massacred a Huguenot congregation discovered holding a service – now perfectly legal – in a barn outside the small town of Vassy. In response the Protestants of France rose in arms, and committed their own excesses: in late April, Lyons was pillaged with exceptional ferocity. Indeed, atrocity and counter-atrocity would be the steady, brutal pattern of the wars to come. The first significant battle was at Dreux on 19 December: a Catholic force – they posed as 'royal' as well – under the elderly but redoubtable constable Montmorency met the Huguenots under the Prince of Condé. Losses were about equal, but the Catholics won the field. Curiously both commanders were captured, evidence of the day's even fortune, and a foreshadowing of the stalemate to come. Two months after the battle an assassin shot the Duke of Guise – in revenge for Vassy. One month later still, in March 1563, Catherine de' Medici helped engineer a truce, which settled nothing.

Hostilities resumed in September 1567 with a failed Huguenot attempt to kidnap the court and force Charles IX and his mother to sanction the Protestant party. The incident only drove the king into the arms of the Catholic grandees, and Charles went to ground in the sanctuary of ultra-Catholic Paris. The leaders of the Huguenots, Condé and the admiral Coligny, settled to a blockade of the capital. On 10 November 1567 the royal commander, again the constable Montmorency, issued from Paris to break the Protestant grip on the

The Huguenot sack of Lyons, 1562. Provoked by the massacre at Vassy of a Calvinist congregation at worship, many French Huguenots rose up to seize control of their communities. At Lyons, where the Huguenots were a minority, the rising got out of hand, and the violence moved from the destruction of church images to the pillaging of shops. Note the weighing of gold and silver reliquaries and church plate in the scene at lower right. The massacre at Vassy and the sack of Lyons were among the opening acts of the French Religious Wars (1562–94).

city. The battle, fought between Paris and the satellite town of St Denis, was another bloody tactical draw: Montmorency was mortally wounded and the Huguenots kept their ground, but their losses forced an end to the blockade of Paris. Truce prevented more campaigning, but war soon returned after another failed kidnapping – this time a Catholic attempt on Condé and Coligny in August of 1568. The next

year the Huguenots were defeated at Jarnac (13 March 1569), where Condé was killed in cold blood soon after being captured. A second and more substantial Catholic success, at Moncountour (3 October 1569), failed to provide its victors with any conclusive political advantage. In its third round the war was still a stalemate, and the only logical policy was another try at peace.

Lasting reconciliation briefly seemed possible, in the form of a royal wedding between Catherine's daughter Marguerite and a Protestant prince, Henry of Navarre. But the royal and Catholic parties chose a darker course: first the murder of Coligny, and then, a few days later on 24 August 1572 – St Bartholomew's Day – the wholesale massacre of the Huguenot wedding guests gathered in Paris. Simultaneous local massacres echoed throughout the provinces. This premeditated horror failed to decapitate the Huguenot cause, the obvious political hope behind the killings. Instead it only plunged France back into civil war – but

The battle of St Denis (1567). This tapestry highlights several incidents from the battle: the royal army is on the right; the Huguenots are to the left, dressed in white. At the centre, marked by the letter L, the Catholic commander Montmorency (wearing a red coat with a white cross) is mortally wounded by a pistol shot. At the bottom of the tapestry a company of Huguenot arquebusiers, marked with the letter K, fire on the flanks of the royal cavalry from the protection of a ditch. The noble cavalry of both sides are of a transitional type. They have abandoned horse armour and taken up the pistol, but not given up the lance.

there was still no possible path to a military victory. For the Catholic faction to triumph, every Huguenot town in France would have to be reduced. The successful but arduous Catholic siege of La Rochelle, one of the greatest Protestant bases in the west, took from 11 February to 6 July 1573: that pace of conquest, one town per campaign year, simply put a royal and Catholic military victory out of reach. A Protestant victory was even more improbable – though secure in their strongholds, the Huguenots remained a minority in the country as a whole. But if neither side could win by military action, a third option – namely peace

The battle of Jarnac (1569). The Catholic army is carrying banners with red or white crosses, the Huguenots white and black flags. As in most battles of the French Religious Wars, the action at Jarnac was dominated by the cavalry. Note the formation of German Protestant pistoleers marked with the letter F. The most infamous incident of the battle is shown at bottom left, the murder by pistol of the captured Huguenot leader Condé. The battle was a Catholic victory, but yielded no great political or strategic advantage.

– had also proved impossible. The only remaining course was intermittent warfare until France reached the point of prostration; and this, tragically, was indeed the direction of the continuing civil wars following St Bartholomew's.

The French wars also became increasingly three-sided. Henry III, Catherine de' Medici's third son to rule France, became king in 1574. He was personally notorious, and extremely unattractive to the most politically uncompromising Catholics. That faction eventually looked away from their Valois monarch and towards the Guise, who in 1576 organized the ultra Catholics into a separate party, the Holy or Catholic League, who were pledged to accept no compromise with the Huguenots – least of all a Protestant king, which became a real dynastic possibility from the death of Henry III's brother in 1584. Leadership of the third party in French politics, the Huguenots, passed to Henry of Navarre, who escaped from his near arrest at the royal court in 1576, and who from 1584 had the best dynastic claim to the throne of France should Henry III die. These three factions – Valois royalist, Holy League and Protestant Bourbon – would come to a final collision in the late 1580s, by which time the French Religious Wars were closely tied to those in the Low Countries.

Over the same years that France first slipped into civil war a similar disintegration beset the Netherlands, ruled by King Philip II of Spain. As elsewhere, there were many causes of unrest and revolt. Several of the leading noblemen of the Netherlands suspected a creeping hispanification in Habsburg rule, and resented the robust garrisons of Spanish soldiers that officially faced France but were a heavy presence none the less. There was also grumbling over taxes – that perennial source of grievance. Yet by far the most sensitive issue was religion. The activity of Calvinist preachers, and the apparently rapid growth of Protestant communities, made the devoutly Catholic Philip and his representatives in Brussels uneasy. Inquisitorial prosecutions for heresy jumped in 1562, and that investigation and repression alienated subjects whose consciences now set them at odds with their king – or who saw no harm in their neighbour's new profession of faith. To further improve Catholic religious control, Philip also sponsored the establishment of new, smaller bishoprics. It is interesting to note that Philip's hard-line policy failed in the Netherlands just as Catherine de' Medici's more flexible and accommodating (or Machiavellian) policy failed in France; in both countries religious war was perhaps inevitable. In the Netherlands the storm clouds broke in the hot, late summer months of 1566, as gangs

THE DUTCH REVOLT

The Netherlands were the dynastic property of the Habsburg king of Spain, Philip II. Fear and suspicion of Catholic and Spanish domination caused some Netherlanders, particularly Calvinists, to rebel against Philip's rule. From the 1570s the heart of the revolt was the northern territories of Holland and Zealand, the kernel of the eventual independent United Provinces.

of Protestant image-breakers swept the land in the 'iconoclastic fury', smashing church windows, pulling down statues and riling the populace. Philip's Netherlands provinces were out of control.

Philip chose a firm, military hand to restore order: the Duke of Alva, a seasoned campaigner who had played a leading role in smashing the German Protestants at Mühlberg. Once Philip decided on substantial military intervention he faced a strategic problem: how to project force to the Netherlands, so far from the heart of his empire in the Mediterranean? The solution was the so-called 'Spanish road', a long and sometimes tenuously connected corridor of Habsburg and Habsburg-friendly territories that linked Milan in the south through Burgundy to Luxembourg and the rest of the Netherlands. For forty years this highway would be a vital conduit for Spanish and Italian treasure and troops sent north to bolster the king's cause. Alva pioneered the route, reaching the Low Countries with a large and well trained army in August 1567.

Alva's Spanish soldiers too often acted like occupying conquerors, and assumed that every Netherlander was a heretic. Their commander was equally thickheaded, billeting his arrogant, often disorderly troops in loyal towns – not a good way to build local support. As captain general, Alva understood his task in stark terms: the 'troubles' in the Netherlands were a question of treason, to be settled by force. To bring the provinces to heel Alva swept up those notables implicated in the unrest, and instituted his own harsh tribunal to judge them. A thousand were executed. There was also military action against the rebels, now led by a prominent Protestant noble, William of Orange, and his brothers, all members of the Nassau family. At Heiligerlee on 23 May 1568 Count Louis of Nassau inflicted a sharp defeat on a Habsburg force of Netherlandish and Spanish troops. It was a fleeting advantage. Alva took personal command in the field, and won a decisive victory over Louis at the battle of Jemmigen (21 July 1568). The revolt seemed to be over and Alva savoured his triumph. At the centre of his pet citadel at Antwerp, built to overawe the townsfolk, Alva placed a statue of himself, baton in hand, crushing a human monster – its two heads representing Sedition and Rebellion – beneath his boots. The statue was cast from bronze cannon captured at Jemmigen.

But truly pacifying the Netherlands took more than a battle won. Just as after Mühlberg twenty years before, a Habsburg military victory did not make for a political or religious settlement. Alva still faced several policy dilemmas; his worst concerned money. To pay his troops wage arrears he forced a hated new 10 per cent tax, the 'tenth penny', on the Netherlands, an imposition which reignited the smouldering revolt. Rebels based in England, the self-described 'Sea Beggars', seized the town of Brill on 1 April 1572. Even as the new uprising slowly spread, Alva was obliged to prepare for an expected invasion of French Huguenots. By the time the St Bartholomew's Day massacre relieved him of that concern, much of the Netherlands had been lost again. Alva turned to a campaign of slow sieges: that of Haarlem lasted from December 1572 to July 1573. Its garrison was massacred. Alva next besieged Alkmaar, but after six weeks' investment his Spanish veterans twice refused an assault. The war in the Netherlands had reached the same unpleasant stalemate – long and bitter sieges, atrocities and indiscipline – as the religious war in France, and at the same time: the sieges of Haarlem and La Rochelle overlapped. Alva's policy had come to its end.

Philip recalled and replaced his failed generalissimo. The war continued, without advantage accruing to either side. Two Habsburg field victories, at Mook (1574) and Gembloux (1577), could not make up for a greater disaster, Philip II's bankruptcy in 1575 – the war was draining the Spanish Empire. In the Netherlands unpaid and mutinous soldiers sacked the rich city of Antwerp in November 1576. For Philip II the war in the Netherlands had spun almost completely out of control.

The King of Spain only regained control with the appointment of Alessandro Farnese, Prince of Parma, as Governor General in 1578. It was a brilliant choice. A complete commander, a technical professional and an operational master who also appreciated the interplay of

Portrait of Alessandro Farnese, Duke of Parma. A brilliant operational commander, Parma saved Philip II's war in northern Europe. First of all, he directed a series of sieges that recovered considerable territory in the Netherlands. Second, Parma's interventions in France preserved King Philip's Guise and Catholic League allies, and prevented any real military co-operation between Dutch Calvinists and French Huguenots.

politics and warfare, Farnese played the game at all its levels. He also benefited from a relative settling of the Netherlands' confused politics. In January 1579 the pro-Habsburg districts of the Low Countries bound themselves together into the Union of Arras. Later in the same month the rebel provinces responded with the Union of Utrecht: under a representative government, the States General, these United Provinces maintained some continuing loyalty to William of Orange (who was assassinated in 1584). In 1581 Parma began a series of carefully crafted set-piece campaigns. Siege by siege, he doubled the extent of the 'loyal' Netherlands over the next four years: his masterpiece was the distant, slow strangulation of States-held Antwerp (1584–5). Parma's blockade of the city included a massive bridge over the River Schelde, a fantastic feat of Renaissance military engineering. The Antwerpers failed to destroy Parma's bridge with floating bombs, and eventually they capitulated. Not a single shot had been fired at the city's walls – among the strongest in Europe.

The wars of north-western Europe now converged. Faced with Parma's relentless advance, in August 1585, just three days before the fall of Antwerp, the States agreed to the Treaty of Nonsuch with Queen Elizabeth of England, who feared the consequences of a complete Spanish victory in the Low Countries. English troops and English money flowed across the Channel, and English privateers profitably tweaked the worldwide Spanish Empire at its rich and vulnerable extremities: in 1586 Francis Drake plundered the Caribbean. To counter this new English threat, and hasten his full conquest of the Netherlands, Philip II gathered an enormous fleet, the famous Armada, for an invasion of Britain. Several strategies were contemplated, but the final plan was for the Armada to anchor off the coast of Flanders, embark Parma's veteran troops and then land them on England's south coast. In the end, of course, the difficult rendezvous between fleet and army proved impossible. In August 1588 Parma's troops waited in their barges and boats, but the 'invincible' Armada was disrupted and chased away by the action of the English fleet, and then dissipated by storm. Parma used what was left of the campaign year to lay siege to Bergen-op-Zoom, which refused to fall. It was Parma's first setback. Philip's incredibly ambitious strategy for 1588 ended as a colossal failure, both at sea and on land.

The defeat of the Spanish Armada also had consequences in France. In 1584 Philip II had allied with the Catholic League and the Guise faction, offering money and military aid in return for influence. At the 'day of barricades' (12 May 1588) the city of Paris rose in support of the League, and as the Armada sailed down the English Channel a cowed King Henry III made Duke Henry of Guise lieutenant general of the kingdom of France. Philip's grand design for a universal Catholic victory was clicking into place. The failure of the Armada reversed everything. In December 1588 King Henry III lured the two heads of the Guise faction, Duke Henry and his brother the cardinal Louis, to the royal chateau at Blois, where both were murdered. Seven months later, in August 1589, King Henry was himself assassinated by a knife-wielding Dominican. All these murders reduced the political parties in France to two: the Catholic League and Henry of Navarre – leader of

Six days before the fall of Antwerp, Parma receives the collar of the Order of the Golden Fleece. This was the highest decoration of the Habsburg Empire; its award to Parma was a clear sign of King Philip II's satisfaction with his commander in the Netherlands. The power and prestige of the Spanish Empire was never greater.

The siege of Antwerp
September 1584 – August 1585

Phase 1

7

Antwerp

Schelde

2

3

2

1

2

1

4

1

3

1

1

The siege of Antwerp, 1584–5

The citadel and walls of Antwerp were as strong as any in Europe. Rather than test them directly with a siege, Parma resolved to blockade the city into surrender – but the wide Schelde river gave the city easy access to the sea. To close that gap Parma directed the construction of a massive fortified bridge across the Schelde.

Phase 2

1 September 1584: Parma encircles Antwerp with a ring of forts and begins construction of a massive pontoon bridge across the Schelde to cut off river traffic. The blockade has begun

2 September 1584: in response to Parma's encirclement, Antwerp's defenders open the floodgates and drown the surrounding country. Fighting and fort-building will be restricted to high ground and the tops of dykes, while boats with small cannon serve as mobile artillery

3 22 December 1584: boat attack fails to break Parma's bridge, still under construction

5 5 April 1585: the first bomb ship sent downriver to destroy the bridge grounds upstream and bursts harmlessly. Parma's soldiers flock to watch the firework show

6 5 April 1585: the second bomb ship explodes against the bridge, swamping the nearest shore fort, killing hundreds and showering the countryside with debris. The bridge is ruptured but the extensive damage is promptly repaired, and the blockade continues without interruption

7 17 August 1585: an exhausted Antwerp surrenders: not a single shot has been fired against its walls. Ten days later, Parma enters the city in triumph

the Huguenots, and by far the strongest dynastic claimant to the throne of France. Only Henry's faith (an easygoing Calvinism) prevented a simple solution to France's continuing political and military crisis.

Already styling himself Henry IV of France, Navarre confronted the Catholic League. At the battle of Arques (21 September 1589) Henry defeated a larger League army, then swooped on Paris, the capital and Catholic stronghold; but his attempted escalade failed. The next year Navarre again met the League army, at Ivry on 14 March 1590. As often in the French Religious Wars, the main contest was between the cavalry. After Navarre's horsemen won the day, the battle turned to the destruction of the Catholic infantry. Few were not killed or captured. With the League field army eliminated Henry settled to a serious blockade of Paris, beginning on 1 May. Over the summer of 1590 it became clear that Paris must fall, sooner or later – except that now Parma intervened from the Netherlands. The Spanish general had no need to win a battle, and no desire to risk one. A defeat would not only doom the League defence of Paris, but risk a States attack in the Netherlands; a double disaster for Philip II. With consummate skill Parma manoeuvred his army close enough to the city of Paris to allow its resupply in September 1590. His mission accomplished, he returned to the Netherlands.

The operational scenario repeated itself in the following year, with Henry of Navarre besieging the League city of Rouen from October 1591. Parma again intervened, relieving the city in April 1592. But Navarre, always looking for a fight – it was to his advantage to risk a battle – trapped the smaller Habsburg army at a broad bend in the River Seine near Caudebec. With incredible discipline and technical skill, Parma's veterans bridged the river overnight and evacuated their positions, leaving Navarre clutching at air. Parma returned to the Netherlands; he had once again proved he was the master of manoeuvre. But Parma had acquired a grave wound in this, his last campaign, and he died in December 1592. Back in France, unable to come to a military victory, Henry of Navarre reached for a political

Henry of Navarre, King Henry IV of France, was an audacious field commander, whose personal bravery won him the love and loyalty of his followers. In this portrait he wears his trademark broad hat with towering plume in Huguenot white.

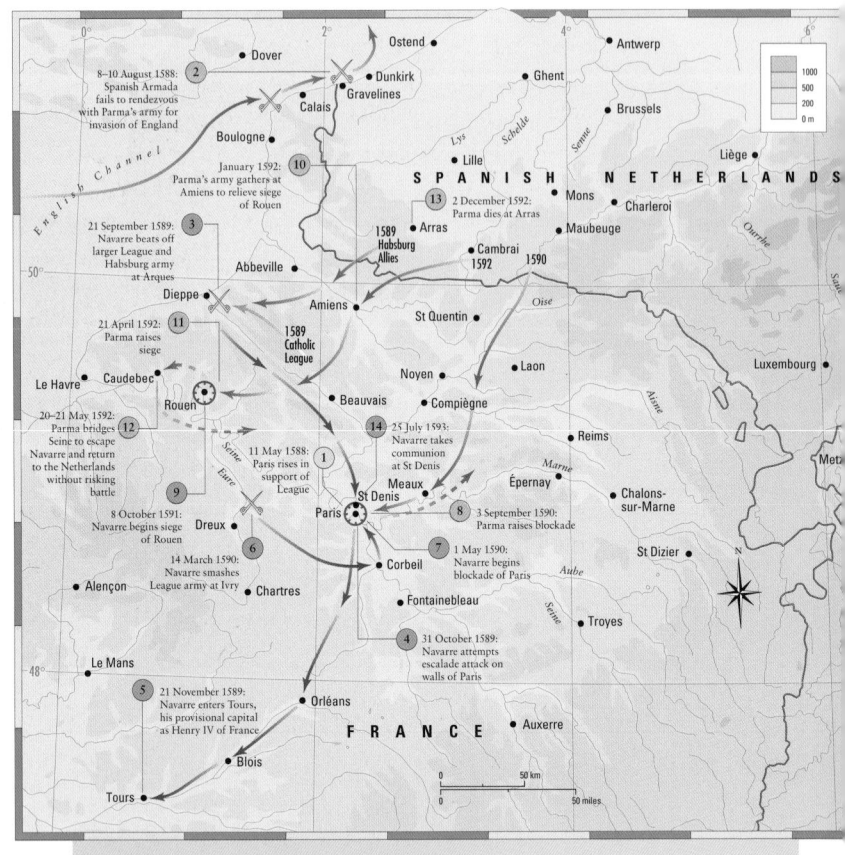

NAVARRE VERSUS PARMA, 1588–93

The destruction of the Spanish Armada meant the collapse of King Henry III of France's accommodation with the Guise and the League. Only support from Spain and the timely interventions of Parma saved the ultra-Catholic position, delaying Navarre's accession to the throne until he embraced Catholicism.

Navarre vs Parma
1588–93

→ movements of Habsburg forces

→ movements of Henry of Navarre (Henry IV of France)

→ movements of the Catholic League

solution: in 1593 he abjured and took communion to prove his conversion to Catholicism. The French wars were over. Henry was crowned King of France in February 1594, and in late March the 4,000 Spanish troops still garrisoning Paris freely evacuated under the watchful eyes of the new king; each marching soldier politely dipped and bowed as he passed the royal spectator. A full peace between France and Spain came in 1598, just four months before the death of Philip II.

The war in the Netherlands did not end so soon. The States had not effectively exploited Parma's French intervention of 1590, but in 1591–2 Maurice of Nassau – the military reformer, and second son of William of Orange – took six cities while Parma was again marching into and out of France. The very real danger to the Habsburg position in the Netherlands had Parma been truly trapped at Caudebec is obvious. Parma's death and an acute financial crisis – another bankruptcy, more mutinies – prevented any aggressive Habsburg action until peace with France freed the resources for a few campaigns in the last years of the century. In 1600 the States attempted an uncharacteristically risky amphibious invasion of the Flanders coast. Among the seaside dunes near Nieuport on 30 June 1600 Maurice of Nassau won a bloody tactical victory, but this could not save the overall operation and the States force had to be evacuated. In 1601 a new Habsburg general, Ambrogio Spinola, began a mammoth siege of Ostend that would last until 1604. It was a contest of superb, almost superhuman effort on both sides; in its excruciating length the siege became something of a war unto itself, a microcosm of the larger deadlock. After the fall of Ostend a further Spanish financial crisis brought both combatants to the brink of peace. In 1609 a twelve years' truce began. When that truce expired a new round of religious wars was crossing Europe, the infant Thirty Years War. The resumed conflict in the Netherlands – now part of a general European war – would continue until 1648. It was only then that faith ceased to be the major cause of war in Europe.

Biographies

ALVA, FERNANDO ALVAREZ, DUKE OF (D. 1582)
Habsburg captain-general for Charles V against the Schmalkaldic League (1546–7), and for Philip II in the Netherlands (1567–73), he won great victories over the German Lutherans at Mühlberg (1547) and the Dutch Calvinists at Jemmigen (1568), but his hard war policies ultimately failed to create political solutions.

BARBAROSSA OR 'RED BEARD', NICKNAME OF KHAYR AD-DIN, BARBARY CORSAIR (D. 1546)
Sailing from Algiers in force, Barbarossa was a serious threat to the commerce and shore communities of the Christian Mediterranean. A Turk and an Ottoman vassal, in 1533 he became high admiral of the sultan's navy. In 1543 he pillaged Reggio Calabria and Nice, and wintered over with his fleet at Toulon as a guest of King Francis I of France, an Ottoman ally.

BAYARD, PIERRE TERRAIL DE (D. 1524)
Known for his uncompromising valour and loyalty, he knighted King Francis I after the great French victory at Marignano (1515). The embodiment of the Valois desire to master Italy, he first fought there in 1495, and was mortally wounded at the battle of the Sesia in Lombardy (1524).

BOURBON, CHARLES, DUKE OF (D. 1527)
After a dispute with his natural lord King Francis I of France over an inheritance, in 1523 Bourbon turned renegade to serve Emperor Charles V. He was killed leading the Habsburg Army attacking Rome (1527), just before the notorious sack.

Charles V, Habsburg King of Spain and Holy Roman Emperor (d. 1558).

Arch-rival to Francis I of France and the sultan Süleyman, Charles also faced the political and military consequences of the Reformation in Germany. In the Mediterranean, he took Tunis in 1535 but failed before Algiers in 1541. In Germany, he severely defeated the Lutheran princes of the Schmalkaldic League at Mühlberg (1547) but could not force a satisfactory political and religious settlement. Against France, Charles held Milan from 1525, and several times defeated Valois invasions of Lombardy and Naples. By 1530, the date of his coronation in Bologna, he was the most powerful prince in Christendom. In his last years political frustrations culminated in a series of abdications. He split his empire between his brother the Holy Roman Emperor Ferdinand, and his son, King Philip II of Spain.

Charles VIII, Valois King of France (d. 1498).

His 1494 invasion of Italy and seizure of Naples began sixty-five years of Habsburg–Valois rivalry for the mastery of Italy, and pre-eminence in Christendom. At Fornovo (1495) he fought his way past an anti-French alliance, but his position in Italy was still ruined.

Clement VII, Medici Pope (d. 1534)

Fearful of Habsburg power in Italy, he allied with Francis I of France but switched allegiance to Charles V after the sack of Rome (1527). He crowned Charles V emperor at Bologna (1530), and in return Charles recovered Florence to Medici rule.

Coligny, Admiral Gaspar de (d. 1572)

A leader of the Huguenots in the early French Religious Wars, his assassination was the first event of the St Bartholomew's Day massacre (1572).

COLONNA, PROSPERO (D. 1523)

While commanding the Habsburg forces in North Italy in 1521–2 he took Milan from the French by sudden escalade and defeated a French army at Bicocca. Humanistically educated, he is supposed to have applied his classical learning to the military problems he faced.

CONDÉ, LOUIS OF BOURBON, PRINCE OF (D. 1569)

A leader of the Huguenots early in the French Religious Wars, he was beaten at Dreux (1562), and beaten again at Jarnac (1569), where he was killed in cold blood soon after his capture.

CORDOBA, GONZALO DE (D. 1515)

Reorganizer of the Spanish Army in Italy in 1495–7, and victor over the French at Cerignola and the Garigliano (both 1503).

DON JUAN OF AUSTRIA, ILLEGITIMATE SON OF CHARLES V (D. 1578)

An accomplished military man, he settled the Muslim Morisco revolt in the Alpujarras mountains of Granada (1569–70) and led the Spanish and allied fleet that smashed the Ottoman Navy at Lepanto (1571).

FERDINAND OF ARAGON, KING OF SPAIN (D. 1516)

Creator of modern Spain by his marriage to Isabella of Castile and the union of their kingdoms. A wily and successful opportunist, he ousted the Valois from Naples in 1495–7, only to partition the kingdom with Louis XII of France in 1499–1501, and then turn on his partner and evict the French for a second time in 1503–4. Contemporaries admired his cunning.

FOIX, GASTON DE, FRENCH GENERAL (D. 1512)

Led French to victory over the Spanish–Papal Army at Ravenna (1512), but was killed in the closing stages of the battle.

FRANCIS I, VALOIS KING OF FRANCE (D. 1547)

In the first year of his reign won glory and control of Milan by defeating the Swiss at Marignano (1515). After losing Milan in 1522 Francis personally led the army that retook the city in late 1524, but in early 1525 he was defeated and captured by an Imperial army at Pavia. A prisoner in Madrid, he signed away his rights in Italy to regain his freedom. Once home, however, Francis dedicated his reign to avenging Pavia. After further failures in Italy (1527–8) he learned to move more carefully, and with the Ottoman sultan Süleyman and the German Lutherans as allies. He attempted, and in part accomplished, a major reform of the French Army with his 1534 legions scheme. In 1536 his forces occupied Savoy, but Milan and Naples remained outside his reach, despite a victory in Italy at Ceresole (1544).

GUISE, FRANCIS DUKE OF (D. 1563)

An able commander who defended Metz against Charles V (1552) and seized Calais from England (1558). A leader of the French Catholics, he sparked the first French war of religion by his massacre of Huguenot churchgoers at Vassy in 1562. He was assassinated himself within a year.

GUISE, HENRY DUKE OF (D. 1588)

A leader of the French ultra-Catholic Holy League, he was assassinated by order of Henry III (1588).

HENRY II, VALOIS KING OF FRANCE (D. 1559)

Allied with the leading Lutheran princes of Germany, Henry seized Metz, Toul and Verdun in 1552. Later defeats at Habsburg hands – notably St Quentin (1557) and Gravelines (1558) – convinced him to agree to the peace of Câteau Cambrésis, ending sixty-five years of Habsburg–Valois struggle for pre-eminence in Europe.

HENRY III, VALOIS KING OF FRANCE (D. 1589)

Caught in the morass of the French religious wars, Henry tried
to chart an independent course between ultra Catholics and the
Huguenots led by Henry of Navarre. His assassination (1589) left
Henry of Navarre the best claimant to the French throne.

HENRY OF NAVARRE, HENRY IV OF FRANCE (D. 1610)

A brave soldier and an effective, inspiring commander of the
Huguenots in the later stages of the French religious wars. He was
also lucky, and he outlived and outlasted all other claimants to the
throne of France. Unable to force a military victory on the Catholic
majority (ably supported by Philip II of Spain), in 1593 Henry
abjured and accepted Catholicism to become king (1594). His 1598
edict of Nantes tolerated limited Huguenot worship in France. He
was assassinated in 1610.

HENRY VIII, TUDOR KING OF ENGLAND (D. 1547)

In Britain Henry easily suppressed 1536 and 1544 revolts protesting
his break with Rome, and he smashed the Scots at Flodden in 1513.
On the continent, however, his expensive interventions yielded scant
profits. In 1513 he took Thérouanne and Tournai and defeated the
French at Guinegate, but a 1523 campaign in France fizzled. In 1544
Henry intended to take Paris in co-operation with Charles V, but
instead settled for Boulogne.

LAUTREC, VISCOUNT DE, FRENCH GENERAL (D. 1528)

Commanding the French Army in Lombardy, he was undone when
his unpaid Swiss mercenary infantry insisted on attacking an imperial
army at Bicocca (1522). He died of the plague while on campaign in
Naples in 1528.

LOUIS XII, VALOIS KING OF FRANCE (D. 1515)

Louis opened his reign by occupying Milan (1499) and dividing the kingdom of Naples with Ferdinand of Aragon (1499–1501). In 1509 he defeated the Venetians at Agnadello. However, Italian victories only created anti-French alliances. Ferdinand of Aragon turned on Louis and ousted the French from Naples in 1503, and, despite the victory of Ravenna (1512), Milan was lost as well.

MACHIAVELLI, NICCOLÒ (D. 1527)

The Florentine humanist still famous for *The Prince* also penned *The Art of War* (1521), a recipe book for practical military – especially infantry – reform based on a careful mining of ancient Greek and Roman practices, and their adaptation for modern use.

MAURICE OF NASSAU, DUTCH GENERAL (D. 1625)

The son of William of Orange was an able field commander and a major military reformer. He defeated Habsburgs at Nieuport (1600) but failed to find any operational advantage.

MAXIMILIAN I, HABSBURG HOLY ROMAN EMPEROR (D. 1519)

An ambitious ruler and enthusiastic military reformer, he was hamstrung by real political and financial limitations inside the empire. His participation in the 1495 anti-French Holy League opened sixty-five years of Habsburg rivalry with the Valois kings of France.

MEDICI, CATHERINE DE' (D. 1589)

Shockingly widowed by the accidental death of her husband King Henry II of France (1559), Catherine served as regent to her son, the young Charles IX, and rallied the royal and Valois cause against the threats of religious war and political anarchy.

MEHMED II, OTTOMAN SULTAN (D. 1481)

Titled 'the Conqueror' for his seizure of Constantinople in 1453, the death rattle of the Byzantine Empire. Failed to take Rhodes from the knights of St John in 1480. Also in 1480 landed an expeditionary force that took Otranto in the kingdom of Naples, a bridgehead for a projected massive invasion of Italy and the West that was cancelled by Mehmed's death in 1481.

MONTMORENCY, CONSTABLE ANNE DE (D. 1567)

A leader of the French Catholics early in the French Religious Wars, he was mortally wounded at St Denis (1567).

PARMA, ALESSANDRO FARNESE, DUKE OF, ITALIAN GENERAL (D. 1592)

Certainly the greatest operational commander of the second half of the sixteenth century, he not only directed a significant recovery of territory for Philip II in the Netherlands, but largely maintained those conquests even as he twice (1590 and 1591–2) led major interventions deep into France to support the Catholics or Holy League against Henry of Navarre.

PHILIP II, HABSBURG KING OF SPAIN (D. 1598)

Philip inherited an immense worldwide empire from his father Charles V, including Spain, Portugal (from 1580), Sicily, Naples, Milan, Burgundy and the Netherlands. In the Mediterranean Philip largely held the sultan at bay, particularly by aiding the defence of Malta (1565) and by the great naval victory at Lepanto (1571). His great albatross was the Dutch Revolt, the central problem of his rule from 1566 to his death, and a complex political issue that defied a military solution. In the late 1580s Philip grasped at a triple victory over England, the Dutch rebels and the French Huguenots, but the destruction of his great armada in 1588 led to the collapse of this strategy and continuing military deadlock in the Netherlands.

Sebastian I, King of Portugal (d. 1578)

Dreaming of African empire, he led a Crusading army against the sharif of Morocco, but was killed with the destruction of his army at Alcazarquivir (1478). Two years later his kingdom and overseas empire were snapped up by Philip II of Spain.

Selim I, Ottoman sultan (d. 1520)

Conquests of Mameluke Syria and Egypt (1516–17) made the Ottoman Turks the most powerful Muslim state in the world.

Süleyman II, Ottoman sultan (d. 1566)

Titled 'the Magnificent' for his glorious conquests, including the expulsion of the knights of St John from Rhodes (1522) and victory over Hungary at Mohacs (1526). In 1529 he besieged but did not take Vienna. An even greater failure was the siege of Malta in 1565. Süleyman's alliance with Francis I of France and sponsorship of the Barbary pirate Barbarossa challenged Emperor Charles V's dominance in Italy and the western Mediterranean. He died on campaign in Hungary (1566).

William of Nassau, Prince of Orange (d. 1584)

A convert to Calvinism in 1573, William was an early and steady leader of the Netherlands rebels against Philip II, becoming the figurehead for their cause. He was assassinated in 1584.

Renaissance dynasts

House of Habsburg

Maximilian I, Holy Roman Emperor	1493–1519
Charles V, King of Spain	from 1516
Holy Roman Emperor	1519–56
Philip II, King of Spain	1556–98
Ferdinand I, Holy Roman Emperor	1556–64
Maximilian II, Emperor	1564–76
Rudolf II, Emperor	1576–1612

House of Valois

Charles VIII, King of France	1483–98
Louis XII, King	1498–1515
Francis I, King	1515–47
Henry II, King	1547–59
Charles IX, King	1560–74
Henry III, King	1574–89
Henry of Navarre, first Bourbon King of France	1589–1610

House of Tudor

Henry VII, King of England	1485–1509
Henry VIII, King	1509–47
Edward VI, King	1547–53
Mary I, Queen	1553–8
Elizabeth I, Queen	1558–1603

Ottoman Sultans during the Renaissance

Sultan	Years of reign
Mehmed II 'the Conqueror'	1444–6 + 1451–81
Bayezid II	1481–1512
Selim I	1512–20
Süleyman I 'the Magnificent'	1520–66
Selim II	1566–74
Murad III	1574–95

Further reading

The best general introduction to the armies and campaigns of the Renaissance period remains Charles Oman's *The Art of War in the Sixteenth Century*, originally published in 1937 but very recently reissued (Greenhill, 2000). Oman's technique was to complement a general discussion with case studies of specific battles. These reconstructions were carefully worked out from multiple sources, and so often remain excellent short studies of each event – but Oman's connections between warfare, politics and society have dated less well. A better, broader and more modern overall survey of the place of war in the European Renaissance world is J. R. Hale's *War and Society in Renaissance Europe, 1450–1620* (Johns Hopkins, 1985). Between them Oman and Hale provide an excellent foundation for further reading.

Without question the salient historical problem addressed by today's Renaissance (and late-medieval) military historians is the debate over a possible 'early modern military revolution'. The original essays of this conversation have been republished as *The Military Revolution Debate*, ed. Clifford J. Rogers (Westview, 1995). The leading protagonist in this discussion is Geoffrey Parker, author of *The Military Revolution: Military Innovation and the Rise of the West, 1500–1800* (Cambridge, second edition 1996). In a nutshell, Parker argues that Europeans created a new kind of warfare in the decades after 1500, and that this new-style warfare eventually allowed the European conquest of the non-European world. The Parker thesis has been most vigorously challenged – see the Rogers compilation – by medievalists arguing for earlier military transformations of similar magnitude and consequence.

What of that old chestnut, the place of gunpowder? The most recent discussion of the growing importance of gunpowder in Western warfare is Bert S. Hall, *Weapons and Warfare in Renaissance Europe* (Johns Hopkins, 1997), which emphasizes the technological issues involved. The best discussion of that most interesting response to effective cannon, namely the angle bastion and the new military architecture of the early sixteenth century, is Simon Pepper and Nicholas Adams, *Firearms and Fortifications* (Chicago, 1986), a meticulous and beautifully illustrated examination of the fortifications of the Republic of Siena from the 1520s through the war of 1553–5.

The only Renaissance military reformer whose works are at all accessible to the general reader is Niccolò Machiavelli, whose *Art of War* (1521) is available in translation and gives a good idea of how contemporaries faced warfare as an intellectual problem.

The best analysis of a high-level Renaissance military and political decision-maker at work is Geoffrey Parker, *The Grand Strategy of Philip II* (Yale, 1998). The best modern biography of a military captain of the period is William S. Maltby, *Alba* (California, 1983), which traces the career of the Duke of Alva (or Alba) under both Charles V and Philip II of Spain, from the Italian Wars in the teens of the sixteenth century, through the Dutch Revolt, to the Portugal campaign of 1580.

There have been several interesting studies of particular Renaissance campaigns or states at war. Unfortunately the Italian Wars of the first half of the sixteenth century have not received the attention they deserve. Incredibly there is no general study, and most specific works are dated: Jean Giono, *The Battle of Pavia* (P. Owen, 1965), Judith Hook, *The Sack of Rome* (Macmillan, 1972), and Cecil Roth, *The Last Florentine Republic* (Methuen, 1925), a study of the 1530 Imperial siege of Florence. An excellent examination of Venetian war-making, and a work which unusually covers both the fifteenth and the sixteenth century, is M. E. Mallett and J. R. Hale, *The Military Organization of a Renaissance State: Venice c. 1400 to 1617* (Cambridge, 1984).

Turning to the second half of the sixteenth century, for the Spanish Army in the Netherlands there is Geoffrey Parker's model study, *The Army of Flanders and the Spanish Road* (Cambridge, 1972). Parker provides a fuller political and military analysis of the Spanish crisis in the Netherlands in his *The Dutch Revolt* (Allen Lane, 1977). James B. Wood, *The King's Army* (Cambridge, 1996) is the first modern military

– rather than political or social – examination of the first fifteen years of the French Religious Wars (1562–76). An account of the Spanish Armada campaign of 1588 which places that event in its European – rather than just English – context is Colin Martin and Geoffrey Parker, *The Spanish Armada* (Norton, 1988).

For the clash between European and non-European, Hugh Thomas's *Conquest* (Hutchinson, 1993) gives an excellent, flowing narrative of Cortes's campaign in Mexico, in so many ways the archetype of modern European conquest stories. The Spanish conquest of Mexico in the 1520s can be interestingly compared with Portugal's failure in Morocco fifty years later, as explained in Weston F. Cook, Jr.'s *The Hundred Years War for Morocco* (Westview, 1994).

Several titles in the Osprey Military 'Campaign Series' treat Renaissance battles: Angus Konstam, *Pavia 1525* (1996); David Nicolle, *Fornovo 1495* (1996) and *Granada 1492* (1998); and Tim Pickles, *Malta 1565* (1998).

Finally, for the connection between Renaissance warfare and Renaissance high culture two works stand out: for painting, J. R. Hale's *Artists and Warfare in the Renaissance* (Yale, 1990) and for literature, Michael Murrin's *History and Warfare in Renaissance Epic* (Chicago, 1994). Also notable is the magnificent exhibition catalogue, *Heroic Armor of the Italian Renaissance*, ed. Stuart Pyhrr and José-A. Godoy (Metropolitan Museum of Art, 1998).

Index

Figures in *italic* refer to captions

Picture credits

Every effort has been made to contact the copyright holders for images reproduced in this book. The publishers would welcome any errors or omissions being brought to their attention.

AKG: pp. 2, 20–21, 26–7, 53, 68–9, 74–5, 91, 95, 101, 105, 107, 140–41, 146, 156–7, 172–3, 176, 212. Peter Newark's Military Pictures: pp. 6, 30, 34, 40–41, 56, 81, 87, 88, 93. The Art Archive: pp. 23, 28–9, 168–9. The Fotomas Index: pp. 32, 36, 44, 62–3, 71, 108, 164–5. Scala: pp. 48, 121, 150–51, 162, 177. British Library: p. 61. Bridgeman Art Library: 64–5, 102–103 Alte Pinakothek, Munich; 114 Private Collection; 119 Palazzo Vecchio, Florence; 143 Kunsthistoriches Museum, Venice; 144 Courtauld Gallery, London; 153 Royal Armouries, Madrid; 170 St. Denis, Paris; 184–5 Musée Carnavalet, Paris; 191 Private Collection; 201 Musée Historique, Lyons; 202–203, 204–205 Musée National de la Renaissance, Ecouen; 210 Phillip Mould, Historical Portraits Ltd., London; 215 Lauros-Giraudon. Niklas Stoer: p. 125. Sonia Halliday Photographs: pp. 122–3, 135, 136, 149. Bildarchiv Preussischer Kulturbesitz: pp. 194, 196, 198–9.

The drawings on pages 31, 51, 54, 96, 99 and 113 are by Peter Smith and Malcolm Swanston of Arcadia Editions.